.hack//

Another Birth

vol.2//MUTATION_

**Story by
Miu Kawasaki**

**Supervised by
Kazunori Ito**

**Illustrated by
CyberConnect2**

TOKYOPOP®

HAMBURG // LONDON // LOS ANGELES // TOKYO

.hack//Another Birth 2
Story by Miu Kawasaki
Supervised by Kazunori Ito
Illustrated by CyberConnect2

Translation - Duane Johnson
English Adaptation - Stormcrow Hayes
Copy Editor - Peter Ahlstrom
Editor - Kara Stambach
Design and Layout - Jennifer Carbajal
Cover Design - Christian Lownds
Art Director - Anne Marie Horne
Senior Editor - Nicole Monastirsky
Digital Imaging Manager - Chris Buford
Managing Editor - Vy Nguyen
Production Manager - Elisabeth Brizzi
Editor-in-Chief - Rob Tokar
VP of Production - Ron Klamert
Publisher - Mike Kiley
President and C.O.O. - John Parker
C.E.O. and Chief Creative Officer - Stuart Levy

A  Novel

TOKYOPOP Inc.
5900 Wilshire Blvd. Suite 2000
Los Angeles, CA 90036

E-mail: info@TOKYOPOP.com
Come visit us online at www.TOKYOPOP.com

ISBN: 1-59816-448-1

First TOKYOPOP printing: October 2006
10 9 8 7 6 5 4 3 2 1
Printed in the USA

Character Files

.hack // Another Birth

Kite

A Twin Blade with the ability to rewrite data; he is trying to help his friend Orca, who also fell into a coma. He teams up with BlackRose.

BlackRose

A Heavy Blade role-played by Akira Hayami. She only enters The World to determine why her little brother, Fumikazu, fell into a coma.

Chimney

A friendly Blademaster and Nova's partner. His goal is to spring all traps.

Nova

A Heavy Blade partnered with Chimney. He teaches BlackRose the basics of The World.

Mia

A catlike avatar who shouldn't exist. She takes an interest in Kite's bracelet and gives Akira information. She is often seen with Elk, a Wavemaster.

Balmung

Known as one of the "Descendents of Fianna," he completed the The One Sin event along with Orca. He's also trying to find information about Orca's coma and believes Kite might be the cause.

Natsume

A Twin Blade who runs into Kite. She doesn't understand how dangerous this adventure is.

Mistral

A highly inquisitive Wavemaster who likes to collect unusual items. Though she often seems impulsive, she is actually quite level-headed.

History of The World

End of the 20th Century

The U.S. Department of Defense develops the ARPANET, which becomes the basis of the Internet. By 1999, almost everyone across the world has access.

Beginning of the 21st Century

As the Internet increases in popularity, classified government information becomes harder to conceal and easier to obtain. Hackers continue to attack networks; cyber crime increases.

2002.10

The United Nations subsystem, WNC, is implemented.

2003.1

WNC winter meeting.

2003.4

A new virus called *Hello, WNC* infects up to ten million users.

2003.12

The Japanese youth who created the *Deadly Flash* virus is sentenced to death.

2004.4

At the WNC spring meeting, the following bills are passed: *Investigation and Research of New Viruses, Technical Security Development Aid*, and *Strengthening Reinforced Penal Regulations of Net Crime*.

2004.8

Emma Weilant dies.

The net poem *Epitaph of Twilight* is lost before it can be completed.

The Swiss Bank's main computer gets hacked, losing more than $84 million.

2005.1

Hacking causes the New York Stock Exchange's prices to hike.

2005.12

On December 24th, *Pluto Kiss* shuts down the Internet; all network computers and communication control systems crash, only to recover 77 minutes later. A 10-year-old elementary school student causes the virus.

2006.1

America's 44th president, Jim Stonecold, resigns.

ALTIMIT OS becomes The World's most commonly used operating system.

2006 Summer

CyberConnect Corporation (CC Corp.) takes over and becomes the foundation for The World.

Harold Hoerwick sells Fragment to CC Corp.

2007.1

The ALTIMIT OS Corporation (head office in San Francisco) establishes 12 overseas affiliation firms.

2007.5

Watarai and Junichiro Tokuoka begin work on the Japanese version of Fragment, which later becomes The World.

ALTIMIT OS' Fragment begins its test play.

2007.7

Fragment becomes the most popular topic among network game users.

2007.10

WNC announces that all computers switch to ALTIMIT OS.

On December 24th, the United Nations names *The Mother Mary's Kiss* an international holiday.

CC Corp. announces the release of Fragment.

2007.11
Beginning of the month

Within the beginning of the first hour, The World receives more than 100,000 orders.

2007.11
End of the month

CC Corp. denies the rumors of discontinuing The World.

2007.12.24

The World's Network Security Declaration President, Alex Coleman, is informed of the start of The World's download sale.

2010

While debugging, Watarai meets with the Vagrant AI. (Story #1, 2nd Character)

Watarai investigates the cat PC. (Story #2, Wotan's Spear, based on *.hack//Sign*)

The second Internet crash, *Pluto Again*, occurs. (Based on the PS2 game)

2011

Watarai leaves
CC Corp.

2013

Saki Shibayama
takes over as
official debugger.
(Story #3,
Kamui)

Rena Kunisaki
purchases The
World. (Story
#4, Rumor)

2014

.hackers Official
Limited Edition
Character
Exhibition.
(Story #5,
Firefly, based on
*.hack//Legend of the
Twilight*)

File "DD"

I felt like a spy.

Although I'd entered my brother's room many times since he'd fallen into a coma, today was different; today I was going to search through his computer.

I opened the door quietly and slipped inside. Hana, my brother's pet prairie dog, raised her head to see who had entered the room. When she saw it was only me she turned away.

"Sorry I'm not Fumikazu," I whispered, quietly shutting the door behind me.

I'd fed and cared for Hana, but she'd been forlorn since my brother disappeared from her life.

I always felt guilty entering his room. Normally, I wouldn't dream of touching his stuff, but today I had no choice. It was my fault Fumikazu was in the hospital. My brother lost consciousness while playing an online fantasy game called The World. It was my fault because I chose the coordinates of his next adventure. Immediately after I left the room, he fell unconscious.

Afterward, even though I'd never played online games before, I joined The World to try and discover what caused his fate. I was horrified to learn that my brother wasn't alone. Others were also being affected by some terrible online creature that could lash into the physical world through cyberspace.

For the moment, I didn't have to worry about that. Right now, my task was easy. I simply needed to pay his monthly fee so his online character would not be deleted. I didn't want my brother waking from his coma only to learn he'd lost his favorite character because of an overdue bill.

Unfortunately, I couldn't pay his fees without his password. I tried guessing, but every guess failed. I needed to search his computer files for some clue as to what his password might be.

Hana scratched at her cage door.

"Be patient, girl," I whispered as I pulled up my brother's desk chair.

I noticed a thin layer of dust on his desk. I used the bottom of my shirt to wipe it away and started his computer.

"I hope it's here," I murmured as I listened to the sound of the hard drive loading the operating system.

I pulled on the goggles and wondered where to search. My first choice was to look through his e-mail. Usually online companies sent confirmations that included both your ID and password. If I could find that message, I could log in under his name.

I hesitated, however, before opening his e-mail folder. I knew there would be lots of personal information, and I didn't want to invade his privacy. I leaned back, wondering if I had the heart to proceed. My eyes wandered over his desktop. Just like his room, his files were well organized.

Suddenly, I noticed two desktop icons that seemed out of place. They were both document files and looked like they must have been projects he'd been working on recently. The first was simply called "Science Experiment 03." It was probably nothing more than a homework assignment. The second document, however, caught my attention.

The file name was rather simple, two initials: DD. What startled me was what the letters might stand for data drain!

It seemed impossible! Fumikazu couldn't have known about data drains, could he?

You're being paranoid, I told myself. However, unlike his other files, which had descriptive titles, this one remained enigmatic. I slid the pointer over the file and double-clicked the mouse. I had to know what it said.

The file opened. The title at the top of the page read "Diary of The World."

At first, I couldn't figure out why he titled his journal "DD." Then it occurred to me: the phrase <u>D</u>iary of the Worl<u>d</u> both started and ended with the letter *D*. Fumikazu had a strange way of organizing his thoughts.

In the upper right corner of the document was a screen-captured image of his character. Fumikazu's ID and password were written beneath. I quickly wrote down the password. It was a date.

I wondered what the date's significance could be. It wasn't anyone's birthday from our family, nor was it any anniversary that I could recognize. *Does he have a girlfriend? Not a chance. I'm older and I still don't have a boyfriend, so it wouldn't be fair. Besides, if he ever did get a girlfriend, he wouldn't be able to keep his mouth shut!*

Maybe if I read just a little of his journal, I'd find a clue. Against my better judgment, I peeked at it.

Wow! This game RAWKƧ! I had no idea how super sweet this was or how many wicked cool people I could meet online. But the game itself is so much sweeter than I imagined. It's so much more real than RPGs. Sure, there's the graphics, but it's more than that. Most games make you follow a path, but not this one. You can do anything! You get to create your own story, your own adventures. It feels so real!

I decided to make my character just like me in real life. I'm a Wavemaster! I thought casting spells would be more fun than just hacking and slashing at stuff.

Shinya's completely the total opposite of how he really is — he's a barbaric

Blademaster named Siesta. Who does he think he's showing off for? ☺ He just told me Siesta means nap. I don't know why he picked such a lame name. Maybe because he's a lamebrain! JK!

Anyway, ever since Shinya invited me to play, I've been hooked!

Shinya Sasahara was one of Fumikazu's oldest friends. *Does the password have something to do with him?*

I heard a rustling sound behind me. Hana stood on her hind legs, looking at me with her head tilted. And then it hit me! The date of his password was the day he brought Hana home!

Hana always held a special place in Fumikazu's heart. When he first brought her home, they did everything together. He carried her everywhere. However, Mom put an end to Hana's liberty after she chewed up the phone cord. Now the only place Hana was allowed to roam free was in Fumikazu's room.

I should have closed the file and left once I'd had my brother's password, but my curiosity got the better of me.

Even though I knew it was wrong, I couldn't take my eyes away from his journal. I continued reading.

I exchanged member addresses with someone new today. I was playing alone and went to a level that was way harder than I expected. I guess he could tell I was a newbie and needed help, because he formed a party and helped me finish the field. He has blue armor and long hair and his name is Sieg. He was totally cool.

I understood the significance of this first friend. For me, it was Nova and Chimney. Who knew how long I would have wandered around if they hadn't approached me and taught me the basics of the game? *But who is Sieg?* I felt like I had heard his name before.

Today I went to a whole bunch of new places. In the last area, we met a half-dead Blademaster, so I healed her. She was really short, and looked silly trying to swing her sword, since it was so much bigger than her. Her hair covered her face, so I don't really know what she looked like. I hope she made it back to town okay. I'm a little worried since Shinya and I nearly died as well!

Afterward, Shinya gave me the keywords for an unusual area, but it looked empty so I left. Right now, leveling up is way more fun. I love smacking down fiendish foes with my friends.

An unusual area? *Is he referring to Δ: Hidden, Forbidden, Holy Ground by any chance?* I felt a chill run through me.

As a test of strength, I tried a high level area. Yeah, it was pretty stupid. At the lowest dungeon, I met Haru, the character I helped the other day. She had made it down there but couldn't make it back J. We teamed up, but since neither of us had a Sprite Ocarina we barely made it out of the dungeon alive.

Once we got back to town, we ended up talking for a long time. It was the first time I'd talked with anyone from the game about real life.

I found out her real name is Chiharu. I was surprised to find out she also has an older sister who plays tennis. In fact, she's a lot like me, in that we're both humbled by how confident and smart and tough our older sisters are. Even though they make us proud, it's tough living in the shadow of someone who can do anything!

Fumikazu didn't understand that I only *acted* tough. I wondered if he'd still be proud of me if he knew that.

I learned that leveling up isn't the only way to have fun in The World. Sometimes it's cool just hanging out and talking—like in real life!

I'd met a lot of different people, too; people I never would have met if I hadn't played the game. It made me wonder if I could have enjoyed the game so much more had I not started under these dire circumstances. Probably not. If it hadn't been for his coma, I don't think I could have been talked into playing in the first place.

I ran into a Blademaster and a Heavy Axeman. They were looking for a Wavemaster, so I decided to join their party. We had to go to an easier level because they weren't as powerful as me, but I thought I would help them out just as Sieg once helped me.

We almost died trying to reach the Gott Statue in the dungeon's lowest level. Fortunately, we made it, but only after they let me rest to recover my SP (that's skill points)! It was the only way I could heal us back to strength!

But after our struggles, all we got was an item called a Golden Grunty. At least it sold for a high price. And I kinda liked playing so close to the edge, flirting with death.

The journal continued on about his adventures and how many times he nearly died in the game. I figured this must have been a boy thing. I wondered if he'd have been as excited if he'd known that someday that game would really bring him to the brink of death.

Finally, I came upon another passage that caught my interest.

I finally saw them!

A long time ago, Shinya told me about the Descendants of Fianna who cleared The One Sin, a supposedly unbeatable event. The story is amazing! Anyway, I saw them.

Orca of the Azure Sea is a lightly equipped Blademaster. Balmung of the Azure Sky is also a Blademaster, but he wears heavy silver armor and has wings attached to his back.

I was surprised to see high-level characters like them on the Theta server. I wanted to talk to them, but wimped out. I didn't think they'd want to talk to someone like me. If I'd been a little braver, I might have gotten to know them.

So, Orca had felt that something was lurking within the game. Maybe they had come to the Theta server to investigate a lead.

I'd never spoken to Orca, but from the vision Mia had shown me, I felt like I understood something of his character. He was definitely brave and selfless. It seemed strange that he'd hang around such an arrogant ass as Balmung, but I'm sure they must have gotten along well enough in the game.

What would Fumikazu think if he knew that I had talked to Balmung?

Today I formed a party, again with two new people (the most you can have in a group). I found out that they're dating in real life. The boyfriend was a Twin Blade named Mac, and the girlfriend was a Wavemaster named Shua.

I wondered why they invited me, but then I found out that the monsters in the area they wanted to adventure in are resistant to physical attacks. They needed someone else with magic!

The boyfriend kept jabbering the entire time, even when we were in combat. I think he was probably the same age as my sister, cuz he talked a lot about school and his part-time job.

I was quite surprised to find out they live right here in the Asahi ward of Yokohama.

During the conversation, I heard a strange giggling voice over the headset, but I'm guessing it was someone in the background where they lived.

Had Fumikazu formed a party with Yuuji and Shouko?! I remember Yuuji saying he'd named his character after the fast-food place where he worked. Come to think of it, I remember them once telling me that they'd met Fumikazu online. I decided that I would ask Shouko about it the next time I saw her.

The final entry was dated the day before Fumikazu fell unconscious. When I finished reading it, I felt like crying. Instead, I pulled myself together and turned off Fumikazu's computer.

Hana scratched at her cage. I opened the cage door and she climbed onto my lap.

"I'm all right," I murmured. "I just want to be the big sister he's so proud of."

Everything depended on me. I had to work with the administrators to find an answer. Of course, it was the same administrators who had allowed irregular monsters like the Data Bugs and Skeith in the first place. It made me wonder just whose side I was on.

Scattered Epitaph

The stars glittered majestically in the night sky. I'd never seen so many before. Living in the city, it was hard to see more than a handful at a time.

Beneath the starry sky, almost like a mirror image, were the city lights of Carmina Gadelica.

I had come to the Lambda root town on Lios' instruction. He wanted me to gather information from the local players in the area. Unfortunately, I didn't know what information I was supposed to gather! When I finished, I was to report to an NPC shopkeeper.

The roads in this town were in the shape of an *H*. I stood in the middle of the horizontal bar. Just behind me, the Chaos Gate spun in circles. Looking down the street, I could see that one side was lined with shops and the other side held a grunty farm. Near the farm, I spotted a local gathering place where PCs apparently congregated.

I decided to move closer so I could talk to them. But what would I say? I approached a small group of PCs, but my courage deserted me. They walked past and disappeared into the gate. It didn't matter; there would be others.

I returned to the Chaos Gate. Looking down the street of shops, I could see a place to buy weapons, magic, equipment, and even food! In many ways it resembled a real small town with its many food stalls. Then I saw Kite walking down the street. I quickly caught up to him.

"Hey! Did you get the e-mail from Lios?" I asked.

"Yeah. I talked to some people, but didn't learn anything."

"Me neither."

"You wanna try talking to a shopkeeper?" he asked.

I shrugged. "Okay."

We formed a party and walked to the nearest shop. When we entered, the NPC roared, "You're late!"

I nearly jumped. Most merchants welcomed you to their stores. But this wasn't a merchant. It was Lios.

"Y-You!" Kite stammered, surprised as well.

"Listen up. I have a new assignment for you. First, I want you to investigate the extent of viral contamination on the Lambda server. Give priority to protected areas."

Protected areas? That means Lios knows that Kite can gate hack.

"To the regular public, these areas appear to be undergoing maintenance, but the reality is that they have become impassable," Lios said.

That's strange. I thought the systems administrators placed the protections on areas. *But if even they can't pass through, then who put them there? More importantly, if they are losing control of The World, why don't they shut down the system?*

"We still haven't identified the source of the problem," Lios continued. "However, we already know your irregular ability can break the protection. And that you need *this* for gate hacking."

There was a long pause as Lios handed Kite something. I could somehow tell that Kite was surprised when he looked at his item list.

"A virus c-core?" he stammered.

Isn't it impossible to obtain a virus core unless you data drained a Data Bug or a monster infected with a virus? How could Lios have obtained one?

"There's no reason to be so surprised. We successfully extracted this from a monster. We found its hiding place in the creature's data before the onset of the virus. In any case, the coordinates for protected areas should be on the BBS," Lios concluded.

Then he was gone.

"Welcome," the shopkeeper said.

"BBS? What's he talking about?" Kite asked.

"I don't know," I replied.

"We'll have to log out to read it," muttered Kite. He sounded tired.

If Lios knew something, he could have just told us directly, but he seemed to enjoy playing games with us.

"Let's meet back here in five minutes, okay?" Kite asked.

"Sure. See you then," I replied.

I returned to The World desktop and checked the boards. I found a thread with the word "New" blinking next to it. It was short and to the point:

I saw a semi-transparent girl at Λ: Dolorous, Evil-Eyed, Widow. When I tried to talk to her, she vanished. Anyone know what it means?

It has to be Aura! Even though she'd been defeated by Skeith, it didn't mean she'd been completely destroyed. At any rate, we had a new lead.

I let out a sigh of relief. Maybe the protection meant she was being imprisoned. But who imprisoned her? Could it be the creature born after we'd defeated Skeith? Whoever it was clearly didn't want anyone coming in contact with Aura. I just knew we had to see her. *She might be able to supply us with some answers.*

I looked at the next thread. It was a post asking if anyone was familiar with the *Epitaph of Twilight.* As I read more of the thread, I learned that the *Epitaph of Twilight* was an epic poem that became the basis for the original prototype of The World. But the text had since been lost.

I knew that the word "twilight" meant things were nearing their end. I wondered if this could be in reference to The World ending. No, that seemed ridiculous.

I continued reading the thread. It had grown quickly since the original post. People wanted to know how faithfully The World was reproduced from the original work, or if reading the *Epitaph of Twilight* gave players clues to the game.

The threads only seemed to ask questions. *Does anyone have any answers?* I thought that if I waited, someone might post more information.

I looked up at the clock and saw that it was time to log in again and meet Kite. I started to put the goggles back on when I heard a knock on the door. Mom entered. She looked at me in amazement. I knew I was in trouble.

"Akira, you're still playing at this hour?"

"Um . . ."

"Don't forget what happened to Fumikazu."

As if I ever will?

"Did you finish your homework?" she continued.

I nodded. I suddenly felt too flustered to talk.

"This is hardly the time to be playing around, is it?"

Even though it looked like a game to her, this definitely wasn't playtime. I was taking chances to help save Fumikazu from his . . .

"Akira!"

I straightened up with a jolt.

"Answer me."

"Yes, ma'am." I nodded nervously. It was useless to object.

"You need to be strong."

I wanted to say: "*You're* our mom, *you* be strong." But I couldn't. It would be too mean. "Yeah, I'll stop. I won't play anymore."

She let out a sigh of relief, but her eyes still looked extremely sad.

"Hurry to bed," she added, and quickly spun around and left. I stared at the door until I heard her walk downstairs.

I couldn't stop. I'd gone too far to quit now. But I also couldn't tell her the truth. She simply wouldn't believe me. I looked at the clock and saw that it was way past my meeting time with Kite.

Slightly panicked, I entered The World, but I couldn't find him. I waited beside the Chaos Gate, but he never showed.

● ⬢ ●

I was cleaning up after club practice when Asaoka asked, "Hayami, are you okay? Did practice wear you out?"

She looked really concerned.

"No, I'm fine."

It wasn't practice that had worn me out, but the fact that I'd hardly slept. I'd spent hours online researching everything I could about the *Epitaph of Twilight.*

Kite never showed. After waiting awhile, I finally logged off and returned to the BBS. I wanted to see if anyone responded. No one had. So I searched the 'net as best I could. However, most of the search engine hits were for sites that had either shut down or that barely mentioned anything about it.

I wondered if there was anyone who knew more about the *Epitaph of Twilight.* Then I wondered if there was anyone who would even tell me about it if they did.

"Asaoka!" I called.

I knew Asaoka was smart, so I took a chance. "Are you familiar with the *Epitaph of Twilight?*"

She blinked. "Hayami, have you read it?"

"No, I've only heard of it."

Shrugging, she said, "I know it's an epic poem by Emma Wielant."

"Then it really exists?"

Asaoka laughed. "I never thought I'd hear you ask about something like that, Hayami."

"What exactly is it?" I asked.

"I read an epigraph in a *doujinshi*."

"An epigraph?"

"Yeah, you know how sometimes a book will begin with a quote from someone else. That's an epigraph. I read a quote from it once."

"Oh?" I nodded. "Do you remember what it said?"

Asaoka fell silent. She was thinking. After a long pause, she finally said slowly, drawing from her memory, " 'The Keel Mountains traversed at last, we met a dragon who spoke thus: "Sheraton am I, who interprets the signs. An answer to my question, give. If you can, complete my role will be, and I will leave this land. Though equally it exists before everyone's eyes, grasp it not one person can. Tell me—what is it?" ' " She turned to me and smiled. "When I read that, it left me feeling really sad."

"You felt sad?"

"Because he's waiting for someone to answer him."

I didn't understand, but I repeated Asaoka's words, " 'Tell me—what is it'? Did you figure it out, Asaoka?"

"More or less. Think about it awhile, Hayami. I'm sure the answer will come to you."

"I don't get it at all." I laughed, shrugging it off.

I didn't want to talk about it further in case the upperclassmen started to get jealous. I knew they still complained about me behind my back, but I didn't want them taking out their petty anger on Asaoka.

Still, I needed to learn the answer. Maybe there was some kind of hint in the game.

"I'm heading back to the clubroom. See ya later," she said and left.

Does she really know the answer? What could it be? I would have to figure it out for myself.

I dragged the tennis net into the storehouse, where I ran into Risa.

"What was Asaoka saying to you?" she asked.

"Nothing."

I knew Risa worried about me. Maybe she thought Asaoka was yelling at me.

I smiled as Risa helped me put away the equipment. When we were nearly finished, Risa whispered, "I'm sorry about what happened."

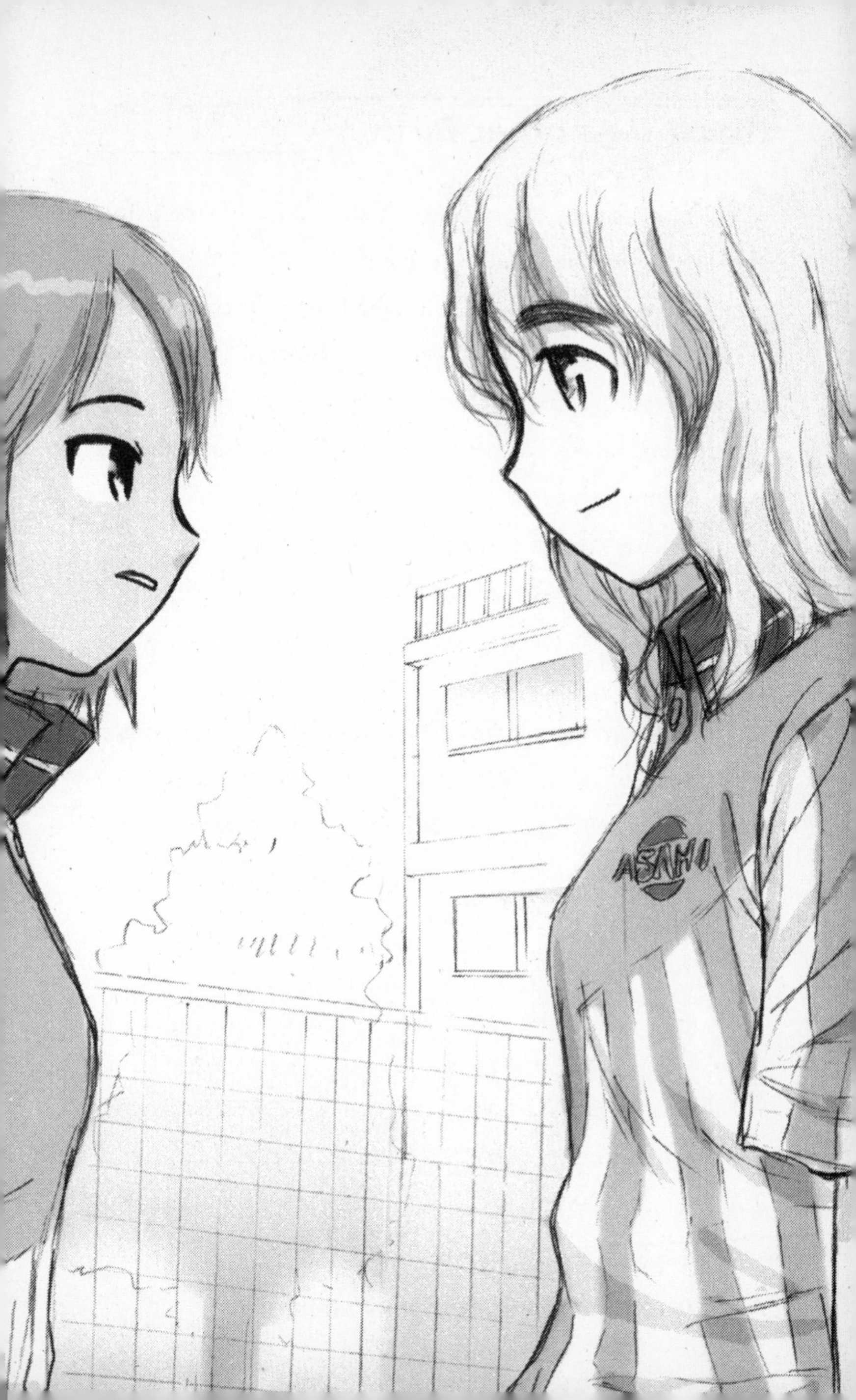
ASAHI

I recalled how bad things had been for me in the tennis club and how much it hurt when she didn't stand up for me. But that was over now. I didn't want to dwell on it any further. While I knew I still had enemies, most of the overt bullying had subsided.

"Everything's fine, don't worry about it," I said. "As long as things are good *now*, it doesn't matter."

Risa smiled, but still looked troubled.

"Come on, let's hurry and finish! I'm starving." I didn't want to dwell.

When I got home, I hurried to the computer. I had to go online when my parents wouldn't walk into my room. I opened The World desktop and saw that I had an e-mail from Kite. I wondered if he was mad that I didn't show up yesterday. I had sent him an e-mail saying I was sorry.

No problem! I ran into Mia and Elk yesterday. They said they wanted to go, so I took them along with me. We didn't run into any Data Bugs.

Mia! She had a catlike avatar and she seemed to know everything. She taught Kite about gate hacking, and she'd shown me what happened to Orca. But because I didn't know what her ultimate goal in all of this was, I couldn't totally trust her.

I decided to take a look at the BBS before logging into the game.

Subject: Protected areas on Lambda!

It seemed like the number of protected areas was increasing. If that was true, did it mean the infection was spreading? If so, we had to hurry before the damage extended any further.

I noted the newly protected area was at Λ: Nameless, Seeker's, Prairie and opened the next thread. Its subject heading was *Epitaph of Twilight.* I wondered how accurate the information in these posts really was. I knew a lot of people intentionally posted rumors and false stories. Nevertheless, I had to learn everything I could.

One of the things I learned was that the fragmentary text data was bought and sold on the Internet. *But how will you even know if what you're buying is the real Epitaph?* Either way, it was too expensive for me. I definitely couldn't afford it.

I remembered reading a fragment of it in a strange room. Though some of it had been unintelligible, one stanza stood out.

```
Shunning the field broken by Wave,
The shadowed girl whispers,
"Surely, I will return."
Alas, the truth unbeknownst,
Awaiting her at journey's end;
Eternal mourning for her land.
```

It didn't mean anything to me. I couldn't connect it to The World. Regardless, I had the day off tomorrow.

I decided that if Kite was free, I'd ask him to go with me to Λ: Nameless, Seeker's, Prairie. I closed with:

```
Don't just play games; get some
exercise too. You don't wanna get fat! :-)
```

• ⬡ •

I headed for Dun Loireag. Because grunties were specific to each server, I hadn't seen my baby grunty in some time.

As usual, it was starving. "More food, I'm hungreeeeee," it whined.

I gave it as much food as it wanted, but it never seemed to be enough. Suddenly, my baby was engulfed in white smoke. *Pop!* It grew bigger.

When the smoke cleared, I could see it had grown curly golden hair, and its skin looked silky.

I remembered Nova telling me that there were three stages to a grunty's growth. I placed my cursor over it and saw its new name appear. It was now a "Noble Grunty."

"Oh, thank you!" it said. "With your help, I have become a splendid warrior! Because of the love and devotion you have shown, I wish you to accept this!"

It gave me an item called a Grunty Flute. "If you use it in a field, it will summon me! Let me pay you back for your kindness!"

At least for now, the creature would be out of my hands. I waved goodbye to my baby, and headed for the Lambda server where Kite was waiting.

● ⬡ ●

"Hi! How did it go yesterday?" I asked Kite.

"We didn't see any ghostly girl at Λ: Dolorous, Evil-Eyed, Widow." And ever since the server went down, Mia's speech conversion has gone crazy."

Kite typed in an example of how the log recorded her speech: Bin E LONG 71|V|3.

"It will probably be fixed once they reinstall the Japanese speech conversion program," I said. "More important, did you see the BBS?"

Kite nodded. "I was thinking of going there now. You wanna go?"

"You bet!" I replied.

"Can Mistral join us?" he asked.

I knew it could be dangerous, but she had fought Skeith with us and proven she had nerves of steel. "Sure."

"I ran into her earlier. I told her to meet us here."

A moment later, Mistral showed up and joined our party.

"We'll have lots more fun today," she beamed. As always, she was cheerful.

We gathered in front of the Chaos Gate, and waited for Kite to gate hack. It took a moment, and then we were whisked to Λ: Nameless, Seeker's, Prairie.

We looked around. There were large splotches of rampant code, and periodically the screen inverted, causing a gut-wrenching grinding sound through the headset.

"Same mess, different place," Mistral commented.

We found the dungeon in a medieval-looking castle. I wondered if we would find a Data Bug inside. Or something worse, like another Skeith.

I took the lead and headed inside the dungeon.

When we entered a large room in the deepest part, we saw a Wavemaster adorned in a yellow robe, swaying before a magic portal. He reeled as if he were about to fall.

The magic portal opened and a Data Bug emerged.

"Watch out!" Mistral shouted.

We readied our weapons. But the Wavemaster turned to the Data Bug and said, "Sorry, did I wake you?"

I was stunned. You don't apologize to a Data Bug; you crush it without mercy.

"He kinda seems familiar," muttered Mistral.

"Let's save him!" Kite shouted as he charged forward.

The monster looked like a giant scorpion. His body was adorned with luminous green hexagons.

I followed Kite and struck at the Data Bug. If we took its HP down to the point where "Protect Break OK" appeared, Kite would be able to data drain.

It didn't take long. Mistral and I used our entire SP in an all-out assault until Kite fired off a data drain at close range.

The green hexagons that were coiled about the Data Bug burst away!

Mistral fired off a spell called GiGan Don that dropped an avalanche of boulders on the Data Bug, killing it. Defeated, it faded away.

Compared to Skeith, this was easy.

We approached the Wavemaster.

"Why do you get in the way? Are you in the way?" he asked.

What's he saying? It doesn't make any sense. Besides, how can we be disturbances after we saved him? Then I noticed his robe.

What I thought were lateral stripes were instead missing sections of graphics. His data was corrupt! He was just as messed up as the field.

"How do you do? Do you have the end?" he asked. "I want the end. Somebody please give me the end."

"Are you okay?" Kite asked.

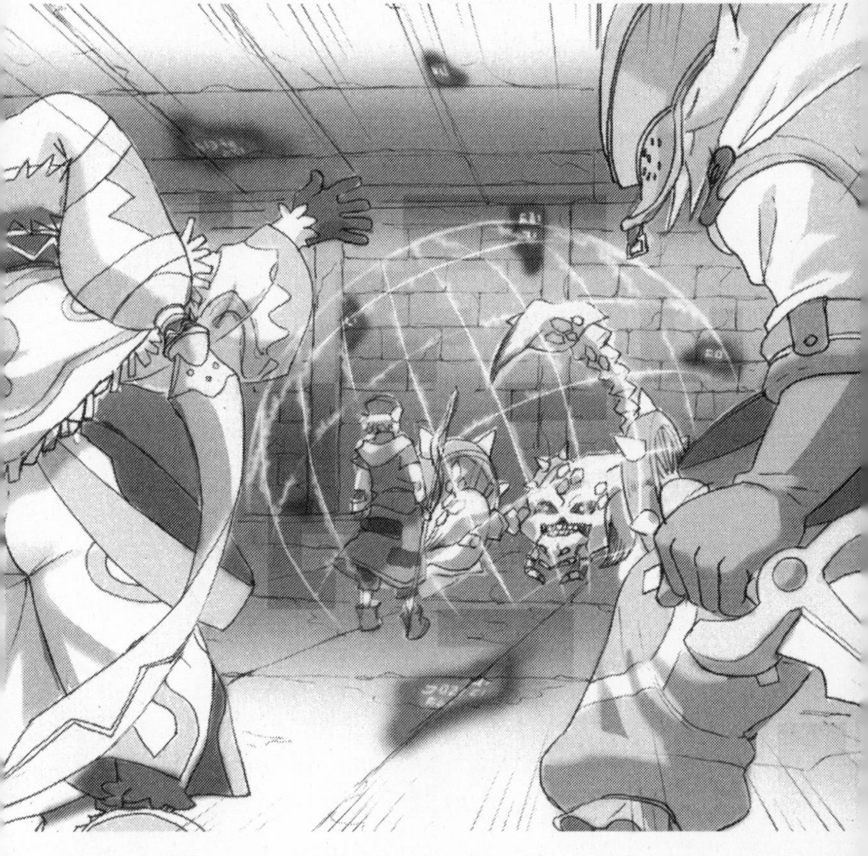

"Hi, we are in the way! Nice to meet youuu!" Mistral joked, but it wasn't funny.

I hovered my cursor over the Wavemaster and gasped. His name was Sheraton.

It was the same name as the dragon's in Fragment. *Can it be a coincidence that this player chose that name?*

While my mind whirled, Sheraton warped out and disappeared. We stood in stunned silence.

"What the hell *was* that?" Kite asked. "He didn't even look like a normal PC."

"An NPC?" Mistral offered. But NPCs had a role in the game. What was its role in this dungeon?

"Maybe Lios knows something. Let's head back to town now."

● ◆ ●

"I've got a new e-mail," Kite murmured when we returned to Carmina Gadelica.

"Well, I guess we'll disbandito for now, but it was fun." Mistral laughed. "Later, 'gators, I'm loggin' off!"

"Ah, sure. Thanks for coming." I waved to Mistral.

"I'll check my e-mail. Wait here." Kite logged out, leaving me with my thoughts.

What on earth was Sheraton doing there? The more I thought about it, the more he seemed like an NPC. If The World was based on the *Epitaph of Twilight* and if he was the Sheraton who appears in the *Epitaph*, then it made sense that he was waiting for the one who would give him the end.

Finally, Kite returned.

"Lios said to report."

"The weapons shop again?"

"No, a peddler in the plaza . . . Hey, think that's him?" Kite pointed to an NPC standing beside the Chaos Gate.

We approached.

"Report on what you found in the protected area," said Lios. His tone was as arrogant as always.

"The data corruption seems to be progressing quite rapidly. We found a Data Bug attacking a PC, so we defeated it," Kite said. "The player was in a protected area."

PCs weren't supposed to be able to get into protected areas. That's why they were *protected.*

"No, it couldn't have been," Lios denied. "More likely a wandering AI. Protected areas have no effect on them since they're botched data. However, I wasn't expecting another Data Bug."

"Botched data? It isn't human?"

"Don't be dense. It's meaningless data; nothing more, nothing less."

Does that mean Sheraton was an NPC whose design was tampered with? I didn't understand.

"We will perform a supplemental investigation. Afterward I will convey your next instructions."

With that, Lios warped out without even waiting for a response.

"What's his *issue?!*" I asked.

Kite shrugged, and I wondered if he realized we were being used? Because they couldn't get into protected areas themselves, they were using Kite!

"It's late. I'll see you later," Kite said halfheartedly, and logged out.

I sighed in frustration. Kite always tried his best to handle any situation, even this one.

I took off the goggles and rubbed my forehead. I didn't like being used as a pawn, and I really felt I needed to tell Kite that. I typed a quick e-mail:

Is it all right for us to go on like this? I get the feeling that Lios is just using us. I don't want to go on like this, do you?

I wondered how Kite would reply.

● ◆ ●

I couldn't get Sheraton out of my mind. The next day, I again headed for Λ: Dolorous, Evil-Eyed, Widow. I felt certain Sheraton would be there waiting for his answer.

As quickly as possible, I advanced to the lowest level. Just as I suspected, I found him.

"How do you do? Do you have the end?" Sheraton questioned.

"We met yesterday. Do you remember?" I asked.

"I want the end. Somebody please give me the end. Will you give me the end?"

I extended my hand and gently touched Sheraton on the cheek. I thought back to the riddle: *Though equally it exists before everyone's eyes, grasp it, not one person can. Tell me—what is it?*

"I know the answer," I said. "The thing that you're seeking is . . ." I sighed when I saw Sheraton's eyes light up expectantly, " . . . this very moment."

Sheraton smiled, then turned into particles of light and vanished. As he disappeared, I heard him say faintly, "Thank you."

He had been waiting for the moment when someone, anyone, would answer him. I'd given him that moment. There was no mistake that The World was influenced by the *Epitaph of Twilight*. This was proof.

I also knew that wandering AIs had feelings, despite what Lios said about them. I disliked Lios more and more. I wondered how long it would be before I would revolt.

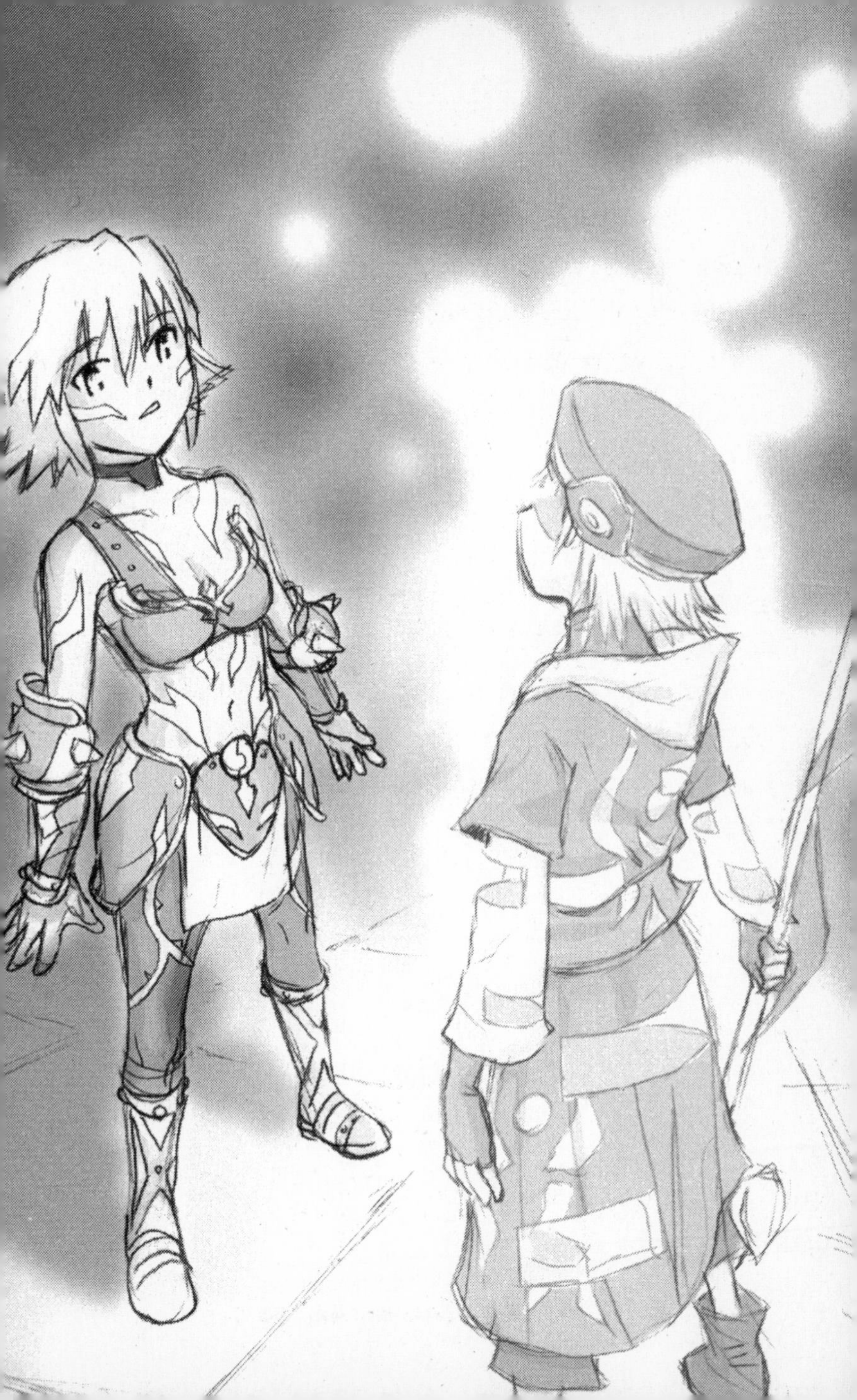

My Will

I wasn't expecting Kite's answer to my e-mail:

`Let's just obey him for now.`

Even though Lios could provide us with information from the system side that no else could get, I still couldn't stand him. I understood Kite's logic, but it still made me angry.

I took a tennis ball from the basket and threw it with all my might across the court.

"Hey! Treat the equipment with respect!"

I jumped in surprise. Turning, I saw Asaoka giggling.

"You have a strong arm, Hayami. You should be on the baseball team," she joked.

"Yeah, but I have no control over my arm." I said as I swung my arm in wild circles.

Once I played catch with Fumikazu and tossed the ball in so many different directions that he never asked me to play with him again.

"By the way, I need to ask you something." Asaoka suddenly grew serious. I wondered if she was going to ask me about The World. "Hayami, are you getting along with everyone?"

"Huh?" I could tell Asaoka was worried about me, but I didn't understand why. I smiled back reassuringly. "We get along great."

"That's fine, but . . . I heard something strange," she scratched her cheek and looked at the ground. She was about to speak when Risa's voice came from behind us.

"Akira! You dropped a ball!" Risa had picked up the ball I'd thrown, and she was now walking toward us.

"It's getting dark," Asaoka said. "You should hurry and finish up." Smiling, she turned away.

What was she about to tell me?

Once she disappeared into the thickening twilight, Risa grabbed my shoulder. "Hey, what's going on?" she asked.

"Nothing." I smiled, picked up the basket with the balls, and continued forward.

"You're lying. Didn't she say something to you?"

"No, she didn't say anything," I said.

Risa hung her head in shame. "Isn't Asaoka the s-same?" He voice shook.

"The same as what?"

I knew what Risa was trying to say, but I didn't want to go there.

"Asaoka is a junior."

"So?" I responded bluntly.

I turned around and looked her in the eyes. I must have been glaring at her. Her mouth trembled. I knew Risa was worried that Asaoka might be bullying me, but I felt angry that she would accuse Asaoka of that when *Risa* was the one who had abandoned me back when the harassment began.

"Just lay off. Asaoka is worried about me!" I shouted. "If it weren't for her, I wouldn't have had any friends at all during the first quarter!"

I felt bad as soon as I said it.

"Sorry," she whispered.

An awkward silence surrounded us.

Risa started to sniffle.

"Sorry," I apologized.

"Why're *you* apologizing, Akira?" Risa rubbed her eyes. "I'm the one who should apologize."

"Stop! That's enough."

"But . . ."

"It's over with, all right? I don't want to think about it anymore."

But it really wasn't over. I still knew the other juniors resented me for being picked for the team over them. They'd probably always resent me.

I took Risa's hand. "C'mon, let's finish cleaning up and go home."

● ⬡ ●

Asaoka didn't show up to practice the next couple of days. It was like everything had changed. Suddenly, the upperclassmen treated me normally. It was strange, but pleasant. Finally, the bullying had completely stopped.

During lunch, one of my classmates told me I had a visitor. Koura, the tennis team's captain, was waiting for me outside. I hurried to meet her.

"Got a minute?" she asked.

"Sure."

Koura walked away without saying anything else. I followed after her as she led me to the clubroom.

When we arrived, she looked around to make sure no one else was there. Once satisfied, she sat down on a bench between lockers.

"It's about Yuuko. She hasn't been to school in two days. I've tried calling and e-mailing, but she hasn't responded. Hayami, do you know anything?"

I shook my head, wondering why she was asking me about Asaoka.

Koura sighed. "Yuuko had said that you were like a little sister to her, so I thought you might know something."

Little sister?

"You know how she is," Koura continued. "She'd see you and say, 'If I had a little sister, she'd be like Akira.' "

"Maybe because I cause so much trouble," I mumbled. Now I realized why Asaoka was so worried about me.

"Who knows? But you're the one she talks to the most besides me. That's why I wanted to know if you noticed anything lately."

After a long silence, I finally told Koura about how strange Asaoka had acted the other day. When I finished, she thanked me for being so honest.

As we left the clubhouse, thunder rumbled in the distance. *If it rains, will we cancel practice?*

I couldn't focus on anything all afternoon. As soon as class ended, I ran toward the clubroom. I heard Risa call my name, but I didn't care.

"Hold on a minute!" she shouted when I didn't stop. I ran through the rain back to the clubhouse. Someone was already there when I arrived.

Risa finally caught up. I motioned for her to be quiet as we entered. I could hear the voices of the upperclassmen inside.

"D'you think Koura noticed?"

"So what?"

"Shouldn't we stop now?"

"Yeah, let's go back to Hayami."

"No, this is more fun."

I felt dizzy. It was my fault. *They're being mean to her because she's nice to me!*

"Asaoka's reaction was amusing."

Amusing? What do these girls think me and Asaoka are—toys? My blood started to boil.

As I took a step farther inside, Risa pulled on my sleeve. "Akira, don't," she whispered, shaking her head. "They're upperclassmen."

"So what? Because they're upperclassmen, they can do whatever they want?"

She was worried that they would return to picking on me, but I couldn't stand by the way she had, and let someone else be bullied.

"Don't stop me," I told her.

"Then I'm going too."

As soon as we entered, the room fell quiet. Three of the upperclassmen: Igarashi, Kobayakawa, and Natori, stared at me. For a moment they looked surprised.

"You're early as ever, Hayami," Igarashi said sarcastically.

"Today Hamaoka's early too," laughed Kobayakawa. They were both juniors who had been chosen for doubles.

"We didn't hear you come in," said Natori sullenly. She sat between the other two.

My hands tightened into fists. "I heard *you*."

"What?" Natori asked.

"Stop it!" I demanded.

Natori stood up and took a step forward. A sneer formed on her lips. "Stop what?"

"Stop what you're doing to me and Asaoka."

Natori glared at me. I stared back. I knew that if I looked away, I'd lose.

"Haven't we already stopped picking on you?" Natori laughed.

Igarashi and Kobayakawa looked pale.

"See, I said we should s-stop," Igarashi's voice shook.

"I'll decide when we stop," Natori spat back. Then she pushed past us.

"Wait a minute!" Risa caught Natori's arm. "Don't you think you're making a mistake?"

"No!" She shook off Risa's hand.

Natori glared at me. "I'm sure it's no coincidence that you got picked, when your dad happens to be a teacher."

"It's not true!" Risa shouted.

I knew my dad would never pull any favors like that. It wouldn't be fair.

Natori shoved me hard.

my_will

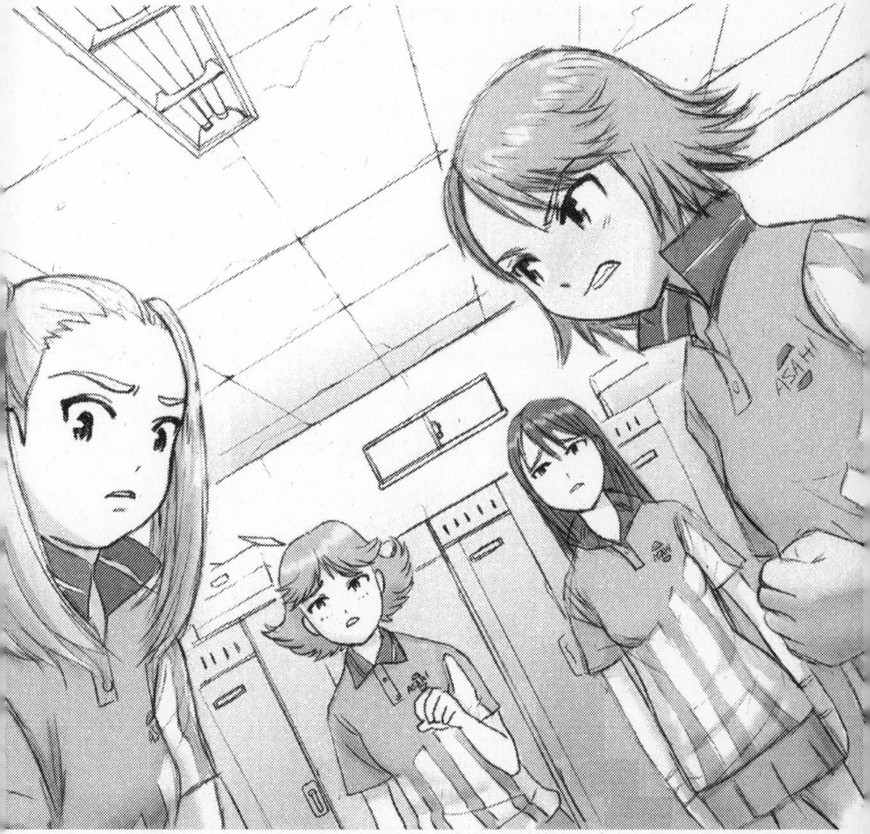

Kobayakawa caught me as I staggered. "Natori! You've gone too far!" Kobayakawa yelled.

Natori slammed her fist into a locker. "You said you couldn't believe it either!"

"Akira's practiced more than anyone else!" Risa shouted. "She practices on her own all the time. No one works harder than she does. She was chosen because of how good she is. I know because I've watched her!"

The upperclassmen fell silent. Only the sound of rain hitting the roof was audible. Finally, Igarashi spoke up. "We've gotten too lazy. We should stop harassing her."

I walked next to Natori. She hung her head. I couldn't tell what she was feeling, but I still had to make my point. "Asaoka has nothing to do with this. I don't want this to continue, and if it does . . ."

"What's going on here?!"

Everyone turned in the direction of the voice.

It was Koura. She looked over the five of us then sighed deeply. "So it was Natori."

Natori still kept her head down.

"Hayami and Hamaoka, take today off and go home."

"But—" Risa protested.

"Go! I have things to discuss with these three."

As we left, I couldn't take my eyes off Natori. I wondered why she had gone this far.

● ⬡ ●

When I got home, I had the following message from Lios:

I have something for you. Meet me at the weapons shop on the Lambda server.

I hated when he ordered us around. Nevertheless, I logged on. As soon as I arrived at the weapons shop, I was offered an item. When I checked my item list, I found I had a virus core. "What am I—?"

Lios interrupted me. "Kite knows the area keywords. That should let you get there. Investigate." Lios exited.

I waited for Kite in front of the Chaos Gate. At this time of day, I expected him to log in at any moment.

For now, I'd go along with Lios. It was the only thing I could do. At least, that's what I kept telling myself. But I wondered if it was the best course of action.

Suddenly, Kite appeared before me.

"Lios told me to give this to you." I passed along the virus core. "You know the keywords, right?"

"Yeah. You wanna go there now?"

"Sure!" Kite smiled and invited me to form a party.

"Inviting anyone else?" I asked. I'd prefer that he didn't, since it could be dangerous.

Kite folded his arms while he thought. Then, he brightened. "Hey, what about Elk?"

"Do you know where he is?"

"Yeah, right behind you."

I turned around as Kite waved Elk over. "Hey, Elk," Kite greeted him.

"Hey." Elk sounded depressed.

"What's wrong?" Kite asked.

"Mia isn't here." His voice sounded small and distant. He was really upset.

"Maybe she's logged out?" I speculated.

Elk didn't respond. He seemed on the verge of tears. "Could we look for her together?" Elk finally asked Kite.

Kite looked at me, concerned. "We need to go somewhere else right now. Can it wait until later?"

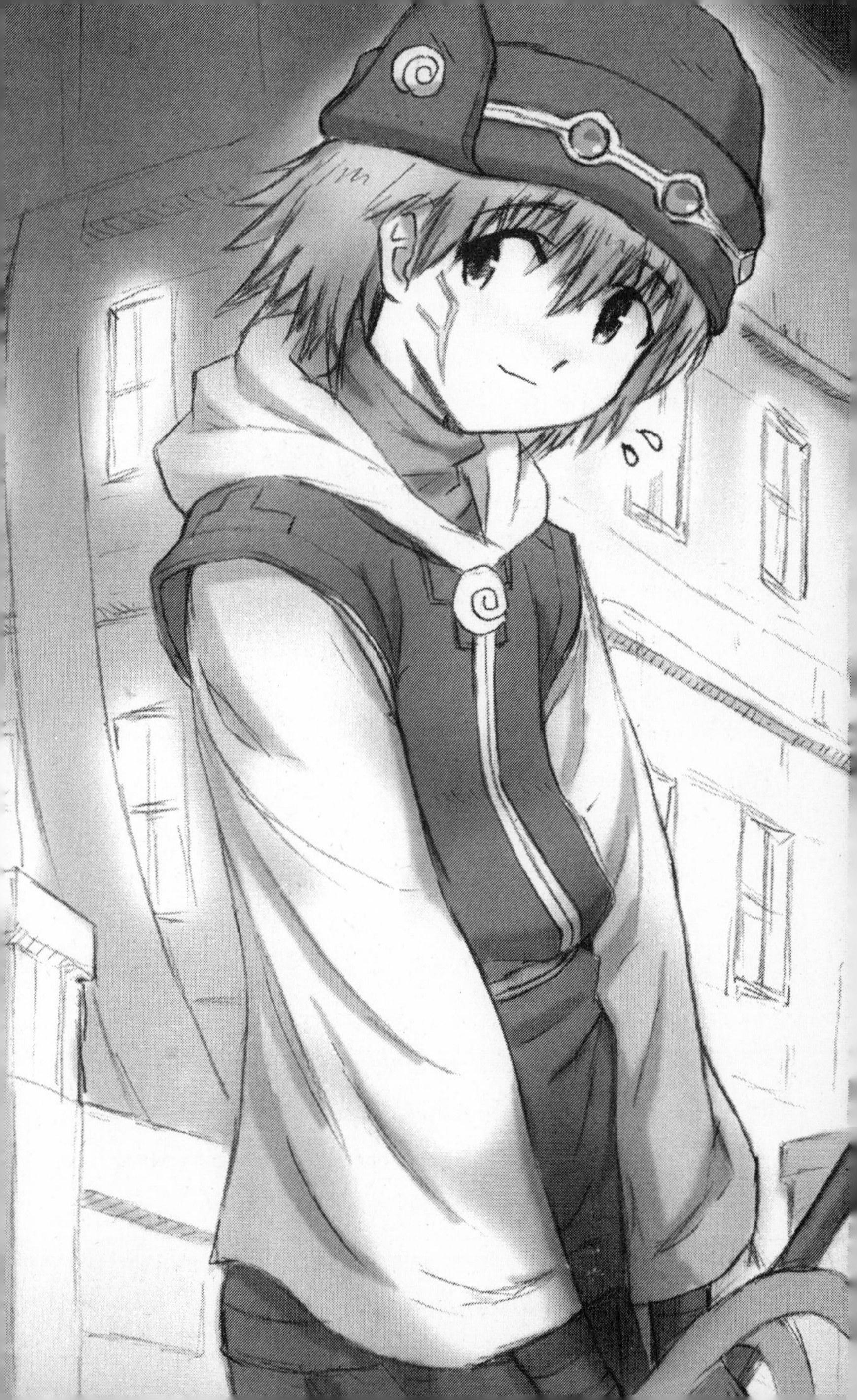

Elk pondered for a moment before responding. "Okay. Can I go with you?"

"Sure," Kite said.

He added Elk to the party. It was the first time I'd adventured with him. I could see his level was nearly the same as mine.

Kite used the virus core to remove the protection and we warped to Λ: Resurrecting, Confused, Judgment.

● ● ●

Luminescent green fissures appeared in the evening sky and red scorch marks covered the plain. Unintelligible character strings crawled through the air.

It was all broken scenery that I'd grown used to seeing.

"Someone's here," Kite said.

We readied our weapons. I could definitely sense someone in this field. Or some*thing*.

"What?" Elk grasped his magic wand tightly.

"Let's head toward the dungeon," said Kite.

Elk and I followed after him. I felt an uneasiness that I hadn't experienced since the encounter with Skeith.

We stopped at the dungeon's entrance. It was in the shape of a dragon's open mouth.

I could feel a rising sense of dread within me. I thought of the names on the pedestal of Aura's statue: Skeith . . . Innis . . . Magus . . .

We've defeated Skeith, but what if Innis is here?

I gripped my controller tightly and joined Kite at the entrance. We proceeded inward.

The inside of the dungeon was the same as the field outside—broken scenery everywhere. I wondered what Elk was thinking. I doubted he'd ever seen anything like this before.

"Let's move forward," Elk suggested.

I was surprised. He didn't seem bothered by the broken graphics.

As we progressed, the noise suddenly became more intense.

"What now?!"

"Why is it so loud?"

Appearing before us was something too inorganic to be called a monster, but whatever it was, it was big. It stretched all the way from the floor to the ceiling with fissured cracks over its entire body. It reminded me of a strange brick-red jigsaw puzzle.

"That's it? That's the cause?" muttered Kite as he ran toward the monster.

Kite's surprise didn't affect his attack. He used Staccato, a skill only available to Twin Blades that allowed them to slash an enemy at high speed.

The monster's color changed to blue. Inside it, a strange red character crawled toward the surface. I tried to look more closely, but the monster returned to its original color, and then disappeared.

"It ran," I said.

"Where'd it go?" asked Elk.

"I bet it's further in the dungeon," Kite shouted. "Follow me!"

We trailed after Kite, heading down a set of stairs. As soon as we reached the bottom, the creature attacked. It had been waiting in ambush.

"Are you a shadow or the real thing?!" I shouted, even though I didn't expect to get an answer.

Kite unleashed an attack against the monster once more. Again, the creature disappeared.

"It's as if the thing's playing tag with us. And now we're It," I muttered.

Kite looked around. "Playing or not, I'll chase it!" He dashed after it.

We soon arrived in front of a suspicious looking room. A purple mist, like the one before the room where Skeith had appeared, hung in the air.

"Before we go in there, let me do something." Elk cast strengthening spells on us.

"Thanks."

"Don't mention it." Elk turned away, seemingly embarrassed.

Is he unaccustomed to being thanked? I wondered.

"Let's go."

We crossed through the purple mist and entered the room. It was pure white. And loud—a screech filled my ears. We must have been warped to another place.

Suddenly, the screen went dark. I heard a splash, and a crimson sphere appeared in the darkness. The darkness seemed to ripple. *Aura?*

The display inverted. Waves of screeching pierced my ears. I closed my eyes, but it didn't help.

When I opened them, I could see purple waves all around me. It seemed as if they would swallow me up.

Suddenly, the noise subsided and the waves drew back. The screen returned to white. I found myself in the room where we met the monster from before. Only now, an entirely new creature appeared.

"I won't let you get away!" I shouted.

"Let's kill it," Kite yelled.

In all the commotion, I didn't know if he or Elk was still with me. Now I could see that they were.

Kite and I charged the monster, but we paused when we were close enough to target the creature. I saw its name.

Innis? Then what the hell was that thing from before?

Kite must have been thinking the same thing. He yelled, "Right now we fight *this!*" We launched a series of attacks, but Innis was too quick. Often, after striking, it would move so quickly that we would only hit thin air.

"What *is* this thing?!" I asked.

"All we can do is chase it."

One moment Innis stood before me, the next it was behind me. I used a Speed Charm on myself and Kite. It allowed us to move faster.

"Elk!" Kite shouted.

Has something happened to Elk? I looked at the bottom of the screen. Above Elk's status bar were several icons indicating abnormalities.

I looked up to see Elk raise his magic wand. He attacked me!

Instantly, my HP dropped lower than everyone else in the party.

Elk was under a charm that induced panic. He couldn't distinguish allies from enemies.

Kite frantically used a recovery item to remove Elk's charm. Once that happened, Elk cast a recovery spell on me to repair the damage he'd done, so that I didn't have to rest before moving on.

I quickly caught up with Innis and attacked.

"Rai Smash!" I shouted. I somersaulted, bringing extra force into my swing.

Innis' HP only slightly decreased. Like Skeith, it was tough. It certainly didn't need any help fighting with us, so I was surprised to see three red dragons appear behind it.

"Holy crap! Where did *they* come from?"

"Look out!"

All three dragons swooped toward Kite. He quickly raised his weapons to shield himself from their charge. Their strike cut Kite's HP in half.

"Ol Repth!" Elk chanted, restoring his health.

"Are you okay?" I asked Kite while chasing after Innis.

"Did he use a summoning spell to bring them here?" Kite wondered aloud.

We pressed our attack. Even though Innis was difficult to damage, we eventually hit the mark.

The message "Protect Break OK" appeared over its head.

"There it is!" I cried.

A magic portal instantly appeared around Innis.

Kite quickly fired off his data drain, but Innis deftly dodged it.

"I'll confine it," I shouted.

The bracelet glowed. It opened like a flower, and Kite floated in the air. Then an arrow of light shot forward, piercing Innis through its body.

Innis transformed. As with Skeith, Innis' substance now changed to stone. It was actually seven stones of various sizes joined together.

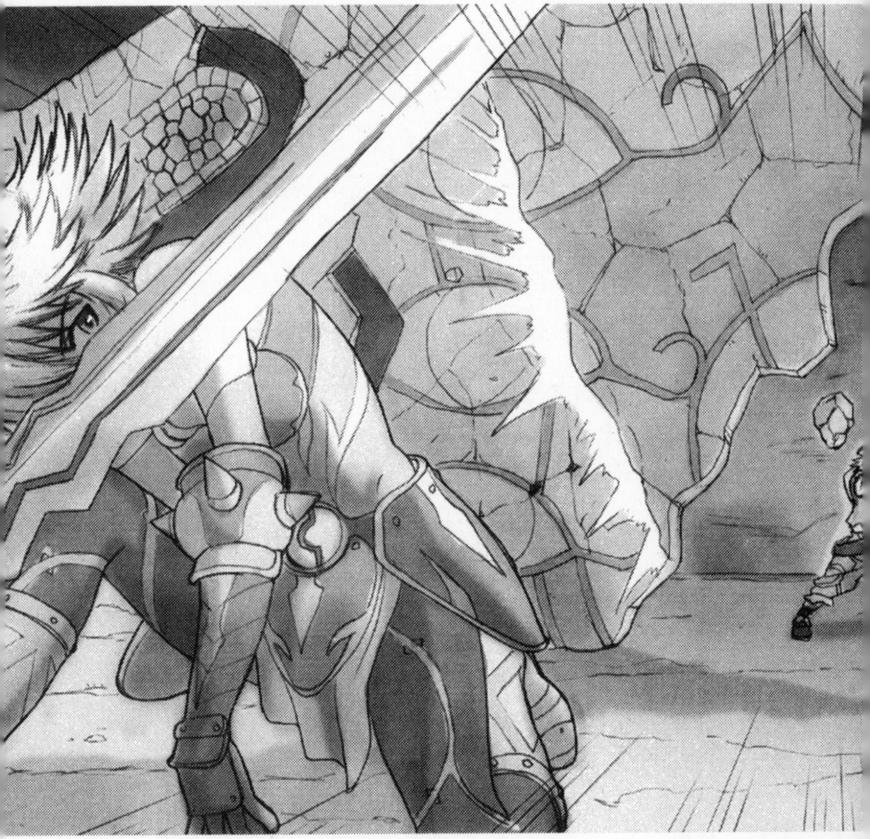

"We've come this far, just a little more!" I cried.

I attacked Innis with my sword while Elk continued his magical barrage.

Kite rushed over. "I got an item."

"Eh? In the middle of combat?"

Kite rejoined the fray. "I'll tell you later, but the item's name is Segment I."

Innis' movements were as nimble as they were before the data drain. Luckily, now that we were skilled in chasing it around, we brought its HP down surprisingly quickly.

Then with another rumble, the stony Innis collapsed. At last, it was over. Or was it . . . ?

The display turned blood red.

We'd defeated Skeith and Innis.

The next one would most likely be Magus. *But how many more after that? How long will I have to keep fighting before Fumikazu can come back?* I felt exhausted just thinking about it.

Suddenly, the sound intensified . . . only this time it was a loud roar, like the wind of a hurricane. *Is another creature coming at us already?*

Just as quickly as it began, the screen returned to normal. We had been warped back to the dungeon.

"What happened?" I asked. No one answered.

"Let's get back to town," Kite suggested.

"Yeah," Elk agreed.

Elk was surprisingly calm, considering what we just went through. *Maybe it's because he's still worried about Mia.* Come to think of it, I had never seen Elk without Mia before today. They must have been close.

We finally returned to Carmina Gadelica. But when we arrived, the place looked empty. There wasn't a single other character in the Lambda root town. "Where is everyone?" I asked.

"Let's look around," Kite said.

After a few minutes, we confirmed that the town was devoid of both PCs and NPCs. Then I suddenly realized that Elk had disappeared. He had left the party, probably right after we arrived. Kite and I were the only two avatars in town.

We returned to the Chaos Gate where Lios was waiting. "It looks like you've done it again!" He glared.

"Where is everyone?" Kite asked.

"We had to shut it down," Lios said.

"Shut what down? The town?"

"The entire server! All because of what you did. It's your fault we're going to be drowning in customer complaints," Lios shook his head. "I told you to *investigate!* You're not supposed to act beyond your instructions! Do you understand? That is an *order!*" Lios looked disgusted as he warped out.

"I can't believe that idiot!" I screamed. "We just defeated Innis. That should make everyone safe. Isn't that good enough?"

"Yeah." Kite looked at his bracelet.

"It's not your fault," I assured him.

"You're right." He smiled weakly. "I'll see you later." He logged off.

I looked up at the sky.

Even though I knew the stars were only graphics, I still found them comforting. They helped ease my rage.

We only went there because of your orders, I thought. *You told us to investigate and we encountered Innis, so we fought it. That's all we did. Then we return to get yelled at!*

I'd had enough. We weren't soldiers or pawns. I hadn't come this far to be used. I decided I would no longer obey Lios.

Its Name Is Cubia

The days were getting shorter. Soon it would be winter. Fumikazu loved winter.

Staring out my bedroom window, I couldn't believe the Lambda server had been shut down. I decided to send an e-mail to Kite:

The time has come. As Helba would say, Lios is pigheaded! I can't listen to his orders anymore! I've decided we should move on our own! Cool?

I went downstairs to grab a quick snack. I couldn't stop thinking about our latest adventure. I couldn't believe Lios! I wondered how long the Lambda server would be out of commission. I decided to check on it.

• ⬡ •

Carmina Gadelica was wrapped in silence. However, it wasn't empty.

The stores were open and manned by NPCs. The streets were full of dozens of PCs. But none of them were moving!

I walked up and tried talking to several. Whenever I did, all they said was, "We oppose support overtime," or, "Opus has rickets," or even the garbled repetition of "Grilnick grilnick."

"This is messed up," I muttered to myself.

The NPCs and their shops were operating normally, but why weren't the PCs walking around? Could they be NPCs? Or was the server still malfunctioning?

It felt like the PC avatars were set about as decoration to make the town look normal; it was anything but normal.

I suddenly felt creeped out. I turned back toward the Chaos Gate and promptly ran into Kite.

"Huh? BlackRose!" he exclaimed.

"Kite, why're you here?" I asked. "Why didn't you answer my e-mail?"

Kite paused. He seemed hesitant. "I got an e-mail from someone else. I think it's from Aura."

"Aura?!"

Aura was data drained and dispersed by Skeith. But that didn't mean she was dead or nonexistent. However, I didn't know that she could still send messages.

"Well . . . it was unintelligible, so I can't be sure," Kite continued. He described the message as best he could, or at least his interpretation of the message. It seemed that Aura wanted us to bring the segment—the item Kite received when Innis was data drained—to a certain place.

"There's just one thing that bothers me," Kite added.

"What's that?"

"At the end of the message it warned 'Beware of Cubia.' "

"Cubia?" I repeated.

Is Cubia the thing that imprisoned her? Is that why the message arrived scrambled? "After Skeith and Innis, isn't *Magus* supposed to be next?" I asked. "Wasn't that the next name on the pedestal?"

"That's what I thought, too, but it definitely said Cubia in the message."

"So what's Cubia?"

Kite shrugged. I wasn't really expecting him to answer.

"Anyway, is that where you're going?"

"Yeah, I . . ."

"I'm going too!" I interrupted.

Kite looked troubled.

"What is it?" I asked.

"Well, Mistral and I . . ."

"Mistral's here too?!"

Kite smiled. "She's already waiting at the Chaos Gate. Is that okay?"

"Of course!"

    [Kite>> wishes to form a party!]

I scrolled through the log, and I accepted.

As we headed for the gate, I realized Kite still hadn't replied to my message about Lios. *If I'm going to ask him, this is time.* "Hey," I began.

"Huh?" Kite turned around.

I looked at him for a moment, but I sensed his eagerness to continue with our mission. "Never mind."

It wasn't important. Besides, I had the sense that Kite wasn't just being blindly obedient to Lios. He had his own obligation to fulfill and nothing—not even Lios—would dissuade his course of action. That was my only real concern.

After all, we were both here acting on our own despite Lios shouting at us and ordering us to listen to him. *Like I'm going to listen to his orders!*

I smiled. Simply having Kite around encouraged me.

Mistral waved from in front of the Chaos Gate.

"Wow! BlackRose is here, too! Yaaaay!" she said. "Hey, hey, don't you think there are lots of weirdoes today?"

Mistral was always acting silly. I wondered if she was like that in real life.

With surprising ease, we warped to the coordinates Aura had indicated—Λ: Merciless, Grieving, Furnace. It was not a protected area.

The entire surface was deep red, and I had the sense that I was standing on magma. Just like the other diseased areas, the screen would occasionally invert, and character strings of unknown meaning crawled through the air or peeked through the ground.

The infection was no longer contained to protected areas. Could this be the result of our battle with Innis? Were even open areas now becoming broken?

Kite pressed onward.

I shifted my gaze to the horizon. The sky and mountains were shaking. I couldn't tell if it was an effect or an error.

We reached the dungeon and entered.

"Goody, let's go!" Mistral's thrilled voice didn't fit the somber mood.

The inside of the dungeon was dark. It resembled a stone castle. Our only light source was the soft glow from the character strings peeking through the walls, floor, and ceilings.

When we reached a lower level, Mistral blurted out, "You've really gotten strong, Kite! Are you trying to be the strongest or something?"

Kite didn't respond, so she continued, "I'm gaga over collecting items. I'm goin' for a complete set! Y'know?"

Gaga? I wondered how old Mistral was.

I didn't think Kite had filled her in on the reality of our situation. *Why else would she still be taking all this so casually?*

We really should tell her about the danger we're in. If we don't, it will be like using her the way Lios is using us.

Still, I was glad to have her around. She helped lighten the mood.

Kite must have picked up on my feelings, because he suddenly spoke nervously. "You know, I've been thinking of saying this for a while . . ."

He looked back at me for just a second, then turned to Mistral and told her his reasons for what we were doing. He explained about his friend's coma, and though he didn't go into all the details that he'd given me, at least she now knew what she was in for.

"Oh, so that's the basis for your role playing," Mistral concluded.

Whaaat?! I thought. *This isn't some background story for a game—it's what happened.* But maybe it was too hard to believe. I'm not sure *I* would believe such a story if it hadn't happened to Fumikazu.

But Mistral had *seen* Skeith. It certainly added credence to Kite's version of events.

"Good luck!" Mistral said cheerfully. "Shall we move on?"

Kite and I were astonished.

"Yeah, let's go." Kite shook his head and continued.

I trailed after them.

Kite suddenly stopped when a crimson sphere appeared before him. It fluttered through the air near his chest. *That's the sphere that scattered when Skeith data drained Aura. Is this crimson sphere a segment of her?*

The segment hovered as Aura appeared in the tunnel. It was as if she'd been waiting for it.

"Whoa! That story you told me was true, wasn't it?" Mistral murmured.

"Yes," Kite quietly replied.

She couldn't take her eyes off Aura. "She's beautiful, but I don't think she's alive."

Aura's eyes were closed as she floated with the segment. Her white dress gave her an angelic appearance.

If the segment returns to her, will she wake up and answer our questions?

I noticed Kite's bracelet was glowing. Kite raised his arm. The segment and Aura responded to it.

Kite tried to approach Aura with the bracelet extended. Suddenly, we were deafened by an intense ear-piercing screech. The ground rumbled.

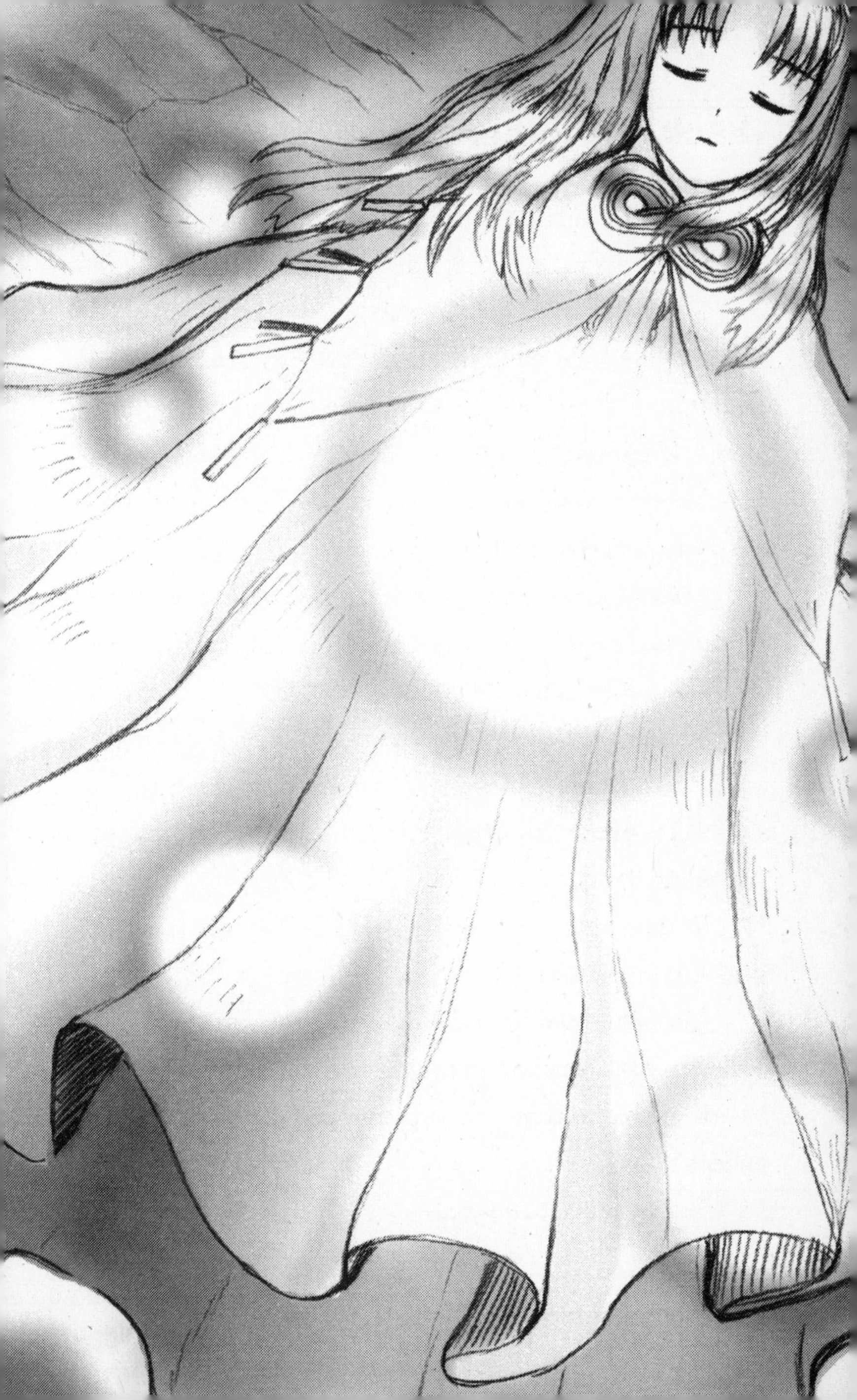

Aura slowly ascended with the segment into the air, until they both disappeared as if absorbed by the darkness.

"Wait!" I called.

"Whoa, whoa! Hey, what is this?!" Mistral sounded hysterical.

The tremors ceased. The ground at our feet flickered and a magic portal appeared.

We warped?!

I looked at the magic portal. Something was inside that resembled the light from Kite's bracelet. It almost seemed as if it were aimed at us.

"That's . . . !" Kite trailed off.

It was the huge thing that was born when Skeith fell. It slowly rose above us, overlooking the magic portal. Its was mammoth.

Its split maw looked like it could swallow us whole. Its razor-sharp teeth were as long as my sword.

How can we possibly defeat this thing?

The head pushed up, leaving our field of vision but revealing what looked like a complicated clusters of roots underneath.

"Is this . . . ?" Kite's murmur reached my ears.

"Cubia?" I finished his sentence.

Mistral cast strengthening magic on me and Kite. I readied my sword.

Deep inside the trunk, what seemed to be Cubia's heart pulsed. Four blue orbs surrounded it, entwined in the root system. When I targeted them, the name Gomora appeared. The larger central one was named Cubia Core.

I decided to devote myself to taking out the Cubia Core, but the second I readied my sword, Kite attacked. Its HP didn't decrease.

"It has physical tolerance. It's invulnerable to physical attacks!" Kite shouted.

"Say what?!" I didn't have any magical attacks. All I could use was a recovery spell called Repth. I wished I'd brought along a scroll, but it was too late.

"Leave it to meeee!" Mistral shouted gleefully.

Maybe I don't need to worry with Mistral here . . .

"BlackRose, over here!" Kite yelled.

I headed for the Gomoras. At least they took damage from physical attacks.

I kicked them around while Kite reinforced Mistral's skill points with recovery items.

Just as we defeated the four Gomoras, Mistral shouted, "It's switched to magical tolerance!"

"I'm coming!"

With my sword poised, I attacked the Cubia Core. Mistral fell back and devoted herself to recovery.

Suddenly the ground trembled. Cubia's root-like tentacles projected from outside the magic portal and attacked. I used my sword as a shield; the tentacles struck once, then disappeared beneath the magic portal. But once was enough. Our HP dropped dangerously low.

"Ol Repth!" Mistral healed the entire party. It wasn't enough for full recovery, but we were much stronger.

Kite and I slashed away at the Cubia Core, but our attacks weren't working.

"It's back to physical tolerance!" I shouted.

"Look out, they're back!" Kite cried.

The Gomoras I thought we had defeated had returned, restored to full health.

"I'll take you out as many times as I have to!" I shouted. I slashed away, but just as their HP nearly bottomed out, Cubia Core chanted and restored both its own and the Gomoras' HP.

How many times has it revived them?

"Deal with this—Flame Dance!" Kite's blades turned to flame and he viciously slashed at the Cubia Core, finally dropping its HP to zero.

Cubia choked out a death rattle as it belched black smoke and sank into the darkness. It left behind a skeleton.

"We did it!" Mistral smiled.

But the moment we let down our guard, light returned to Cubia's eyes. It soared into the air. An intense roar bellowed. The sky inverted, swallowing up Cubia.

It ran away!

I didn't take my eyes away from the spot where it had disappeared. I was afraid it might return.

"I'm impressed. You managed to repel Cubia."

I turned, surprised to see Helba. How long had she been there?!

"Miss Helba." I could tell Kite chose his words carefully.

"You can drop the 'Miss' routine. Right now we must liberate Aura."

"Will that help save Orca?"

"It's a question of probability. For now, that is all I can say." Helba warped out.

If we liberate Aura, will Fumikazu be saved?! Even if there was only a possibility, we had to pursue it.

As we headed back, I noticed Mistral was unusually silent.

"Mistral, are you okay?"

She nodded.

Once we returned to Carmina Gadelica, Mistral pulled Kite aside.

"I'm sorry I made fun of you. You know me, that's just how I am."

I stepped farther back; I didn't want to invade their privacy. But it was nice that she could apologize so openly. So far, I hadn't told anyone about Fumikazu. I wish I could be as open.

"I know you're trying hard, so I won't say good luck. But call me when you need me. No need to hold back. If there's anything I can do, I'll do it!" Mistral offered.

I never thought Mistral would become someone we could rely on.

"Well, I'm going shopping," Mistral said, and warped out.

Shopping! At this hour? I became more curious about her real life. Maybe she was just a student heading to a local convenience store. Or maybe she was going to shop online. Who could tell?

Kite let out a big sigh. He turned to me and smiled.

I decided it was time to tell him the truth about my brother. But just as I was about to speak, I heard something outside of the game. I lifted the goggles.

Downstairs I could hear clattering and Kouta shouting. I had to get down there immediately.

"Sorry, I have to go," I said, and quickly logged out.

• ⬢ •

I heard my mom walking upstairs. I quickly double-clicked my homework file.

Mom opened the door without knocking. I could see her looking over my shoulder to see what I was working on.

"Sorry to interrupt your homework."

"It's okay." I turned toward her. "What's up?"

"Hana's gotten loose. Could you help find her?"

"Hana?" *Did I forget to shut the cage door yesterday?* I shot up out of my chair.

"Kou left the bedroom door open and she got away. You know how fast she is. Kou wasn't able to catch her."

Mom's hand rubbed her temple. She was having a bad day.

I rolled up my sleeves. "If I can't catch her, who can?" I laughed.

"Thanks. She shouldn't have gotten outside, so she must be around here somewhere. Can you look in the bedrooms?"

"Roger!" I answered with a salute.

"And be serious?" Mom headed downstairs to search the kitchen again.

I decided to start by checking all of her favorite hiding places: Dad's study, my parents' bedroom, Fumikazu's room, the bathroom.

Not a trace.

Then I went from room to room. Still nothing. Finally, I heard Kouta calling from downstairs.

"Found her!"

I ran down the steps. "Where, where?"

Kouta held his finger over his mouth so Mom and I would be quiet. Then he whispered, "Over there."

Hana was sitting on the entryway mat. As soon as I saw her, my heart tightened. I realized she was waiting for Fumikazu to come home.

It seemed cruel to catch her and put her back in her cage.

"Akira," Mom softly called.

"Hurry, hurry!" Kouta stamped his feet.

"Quietly, Kou," Mom soothed, but Hana didn't flinch.

I slowly approached Hana, ready to grab her. As I neared, Hana stood upright. Outside, we could hear keys jingling. It was Dad.

"I'm home," Dad called as he pushed open the door.

Hana bolted in the opposite direction, weaving expertly between our feet. She disappeared down the hall.

"What the . . . ?!" Dad cried. Once we told him what happened, he announced, "That's easy. I'll catch her."

Dad set down his briefcase and headed toward the kitchen. "I bet she's hungry. She probably went to the kitchen."

Mom and Dad searched the first floor while Kouta and I returned to the second.

I sent Kouta to my parents' bedroom so he'd be out of the way. Then I headed back toward Fumikazu's room.

I turned on the light. The room felt cold. I looked under the desk and in the closet. She wasn't there. Maybe she was downstairs after all. I started to leave the room when I heard something under the bed. I dropped down and peeked under it.

Hana was curled up in a piece of cloth, sleeping. Hana always snored when she slept. I grabbed the sides of the cloth she was nestled in and dragged it out. Waking her gently, I picked her up and cuddled her in my arms. Hana nudged my cheek with her nose.

Then I realized what Hana was sleeping in. It was Fumikazu's favorite blanket.

A tear raced down my cheek. It was the first of many.

After we repelled Cubia, Carmina Gadelica returned to its former liveliness. It seemed to have been fully restored.

"Miss BlackRooose!" Natsume called. "I was just about to go!"

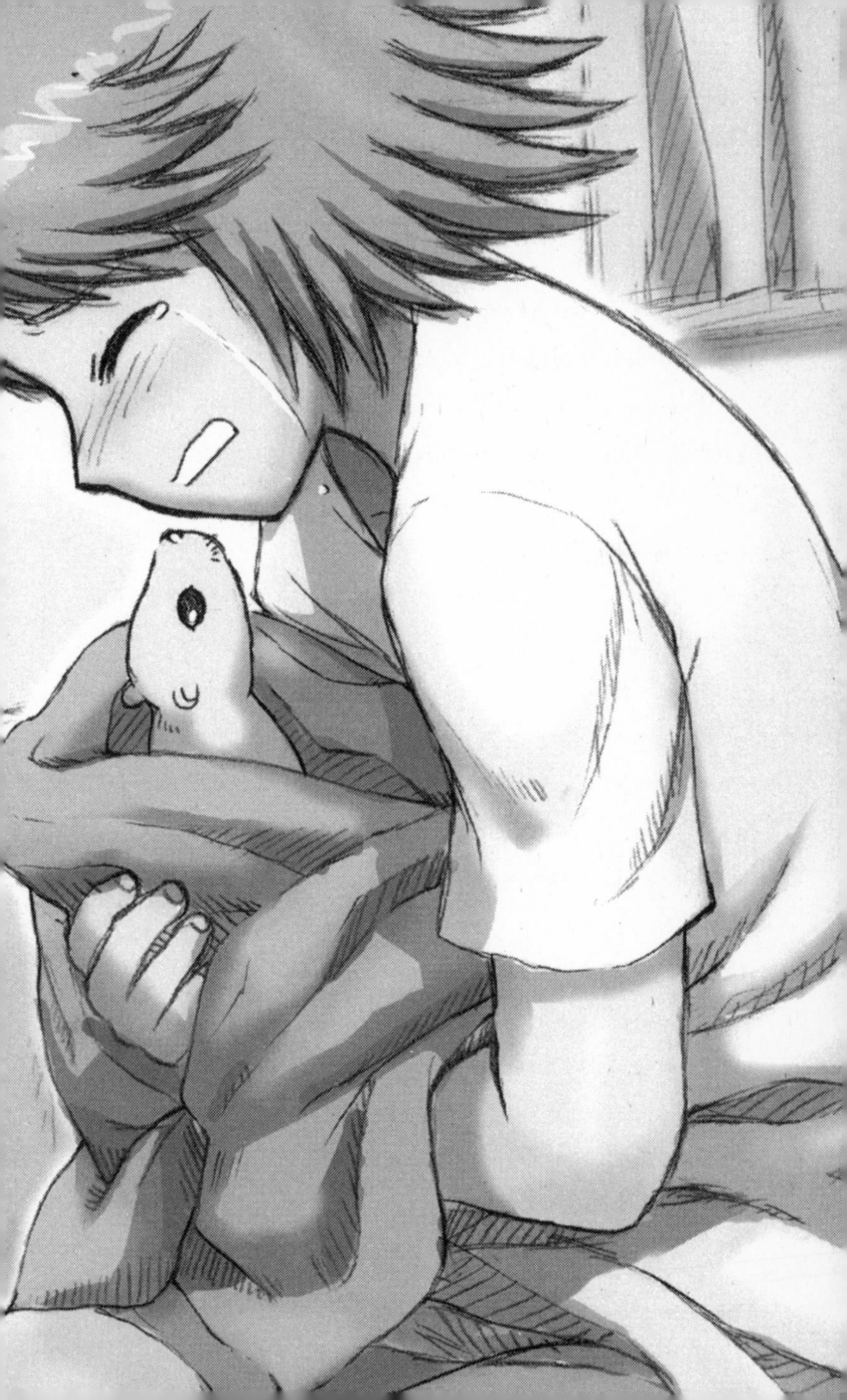

"You're really going?" I asked.

"By the time I return, I will be ten times my level."

Natsume sent me an e-mail telling me about a new post on the BBS. I didn't trust it.

The post claimed that if you defeated a monster called "Level 10 Vine" in the lowest level of the dungeon located at Λ: Bottomless, Hopeless, Footstep, your level would increase by tenfold. Everything about the post sounded bogus.

"It's too good to be true. Forget about it." I didn't want to see her disappointed.

Natsume looked at me in surprise. "What if you're wrong? I have to find out if it's true!"

"Okay, good luck." I waved as Natsume warped through the Chaos Gate.

I decided to do some research. I chose the keywords from the Chaos Gate generator. Λ: Bottomless, Hopeless, Footstep was a level 36 area. I didn't know Natsume's current level, but I knew it wasn't high enough. Even I would have trouble in that field alone.

I started to worry. *What should I do?* I closed the menu, and saw Kite walking past. *Such good fortune!*

"You! Come with me," I ordered.

"Sure, but I wanted to check something out on my own first."

"No time," I said, and then briefly told him about the e-mail from Natsume.

"You, too? That's where I was just heading," Kite smiled. Natsume had sent him the same e-mail and he wanted to check on the validity of the post as well.

We warped to Λ: Bottomless, Hopeless, Footstep, and headed straight for the dungeon.

As we walked under the full moon, I commented, "How long has it been since you and I went to an *ordinary* area?"

Kite just laughed. Nothing we did was ever ordinary, of course.

The dungeon was unexpectedly large. We pressed forward as fast as we could until we arrived at the second level. There, we found Natsume. She was outnumbered, surrounded by hideous looking mushroom monsters.

"We have to help her!" I cried.

We unleashed an attack, quickly dropping the mushroom monsters under our onslaught.

It didn't take too long, thank goodness.

When it was over, Natsume sheepishly approached us. With her head bowed, she said, "I looked in every corner of the dungeon, but the Level 10 Vine monster is nowhere to be found."

Of course not.

"I think that post was probably a joke," Kite offered, trying to sound gentle.

"Yeah, you must be right," Natsume said. She looked a little chagrined. "You ended up helping me out again."

"Our pleasure." I nodded.

She broke out into a huge smile. "Tee-hee-hee! Well, in time I'll get stronger! I will do my best and not fall for these stupid posts anymore! There are no quick fixes, right? After all—the harder you work, the bigger the reward, right?"

With that, Natsume warped out. She must have felt embarrassed for believing the post.

Kite and I looked at each other. There was no point in staying, so we headed back as well.

I wondered what kind of person would leave such a ridiculous post in the first place, but realized there were all kinds of people on the 'net, just as there were in real life. If

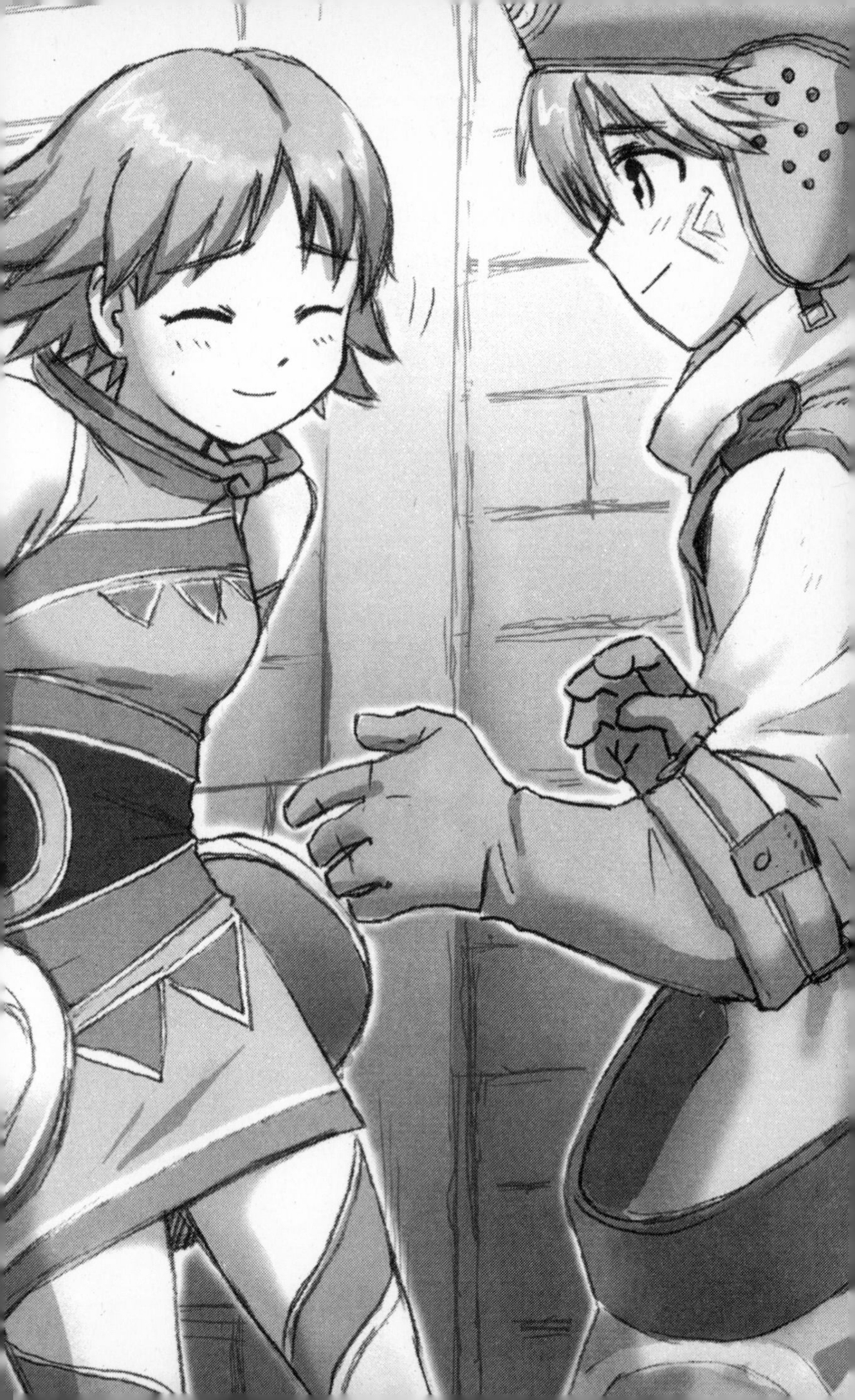

you didn't want to be fooled, you had to learn to be a good judge of character.

I'd learned so much since I'd entered The World. No matter what, I was grateful that I'd played the game.

Fellow

After defeating Cubia, Aura was still nowhere to be found, and we had no clue what to do next.

What would Fumikazu do if he were me? He was more gifted at solving puzzles than I was.

We had defeated Skeith and Innis. That left Magus. *When will it show?*

The pedestal of the statue was defaced, so we couldn't read beyond Magus. *Will there be others?* I had no doubt there would be.

Then there was Cubia. *Why did it run from us?* That meant we'd have to fight it again.

If Aura's segment was a part or fragment of her, then maybe the three red lights Skeith had scattered were the essence of Aura herself. That meant there were two more segments. *If we gather those, will Aura return? Where can those other two segments be hidden?*

I wasn't counting on information from the system side anymore. Lios proved to be too difficult. My primary source of information would be the BBS. I could also talk to Asaoka, Yuuji, and others from school.

Unfortunately, the BBS had been suspended since the defeat of Innis. Also, I couldn't just blatantly talk to Asaoka or Yuuji, since they didn't even know I played online. Nor did I want them to know.

What can I do?

It was getting cold out. Wracked by worries, I visited my brother in the hospital. I told him everything I'd been through these past few days, hoping for some sort of inspiration, but none ever came.

Once I'd arrived home, I made some hot cocoa and hurried upstairs to my computer. I prayed that the BBS had been reinstated. I was really relieved to see that it was finally back online.

Confusion over the downed server had increased the number of posts. My eyes ran over the new responses. I found a rumor about the "coma game."

I wondered what would happen if I posted everything I knew. Maybe then others would avoid irregular monsters. I could warn The World.

No. Nobody will believe me. Not only that, but once Lios learned of the post's existence, he would almost certainly delete it.

There was a new response in the *Epitaph of Twilight* thread. I clicked it and found a piece written about The World being ruined by the "Abominable Wave," unless someone could find the Twilight Dragon, the destined savior of The World.

The Twilight Dragon?! Linda used that expression, right? She'd said, "May the Twilight Dragon's divine protection be with you."

If Linda knew of the Twilight Dragon, then she also probably knew about the *Epitaph of Twilight* as well. *But where did she learn about it?*

Any 'net searches I made didn't reveal any hits. It was also the first time I'd heard the words Abominable Wave.

Before Innis appeared, I saw waves rippling across the display. *Are those the waves?*

I decided to write to the author of the thread.

I wanted to know their source. The author's name was simply 01.

Afterward, I sent an e-mail to Kite telling him the BBS was reinstated and pointing out 01's post.

The problem with using e-mail was waiting for an answer. Even if I hadn't alerted Kite, I know he'd check the BBS anyway. But I wanted to e-mail him. I wanted the connection to him, perhaps.

I decided to wait for him in The World.

• ◆ •

As soon as I arrived, Chimney started manically circling around me.

"Oh! *This* is the server you've been on!" Chimney cried gleefully. "Ho ho! You've gone up a few levels!"

I couldn't help wondering at his abundant energy. He reminded me of a little kid.

"It's been a long time." I said. I hadn't seen Chimney or Nova since Skeith was defeated. I guess I kind of missed them. "Where's Nova?"

"Shopping."

"Preparing to adventure?"

"We actually just got back."

"Then why are you shopping?"

"The SP of two Blademasters doesn't cut it for recovery. So we need more healing potions and whatnot."

"Were you nearly killed?"

"We ran away."

"Is that possible?" I asked.

"It wasn't a dungeon, so we weren't hemmed in. We were in a field, so we were able to shake them off," Chimney continued.

"So you can avoid monsters in fields?"

"Yup. It's lame, but if you call it a tactical retreat, it makes it cooler!" Chimney looked away. "Oh, here he comes!"

"Well, if it isn't BlackRose." Nova waved. "Is this the server you've been on?"

"That's what Chimney just said."

"Hey, you've gone up a few levels."

"I said that, too." Chimney pouted exaggeratedly.

"Then, did he ask you . . . ?"

"Ask what?" I pressed, curious.

"Want to level up with us?"

"Really?" I smiled.

"If you have nothing planned, why not?"

I had intended to wait for Kite. I wanted to talk to him about my e-mail to 01. Nova seemed to catch on to my ambivalence. "Ah, you're probably too busy."

"What do you mean?" Chimney jumped in.

I felt certain Nova suspected something. They had seen Mia, an irregular PC, approach me. I almost felt like telling them what was happening.

"Did I say something wrong?" Nova asked Chimney.

"You did—you sound like some old lady."

"Well, you know I'm not. I'm just short of being a middle-aged *man*," he joked.

"That's okay," Chimney said. "We're just jealous since you're always surrounded by such colorful characters."

"We don't have that many chances to play together," Nova added.

"Yeah, Nova's a pretty lonely guy," Chimney teased.

"Cut it out," Nova snapped. Then turning back to me he said, "When you do have time, we should adventure together, okay?

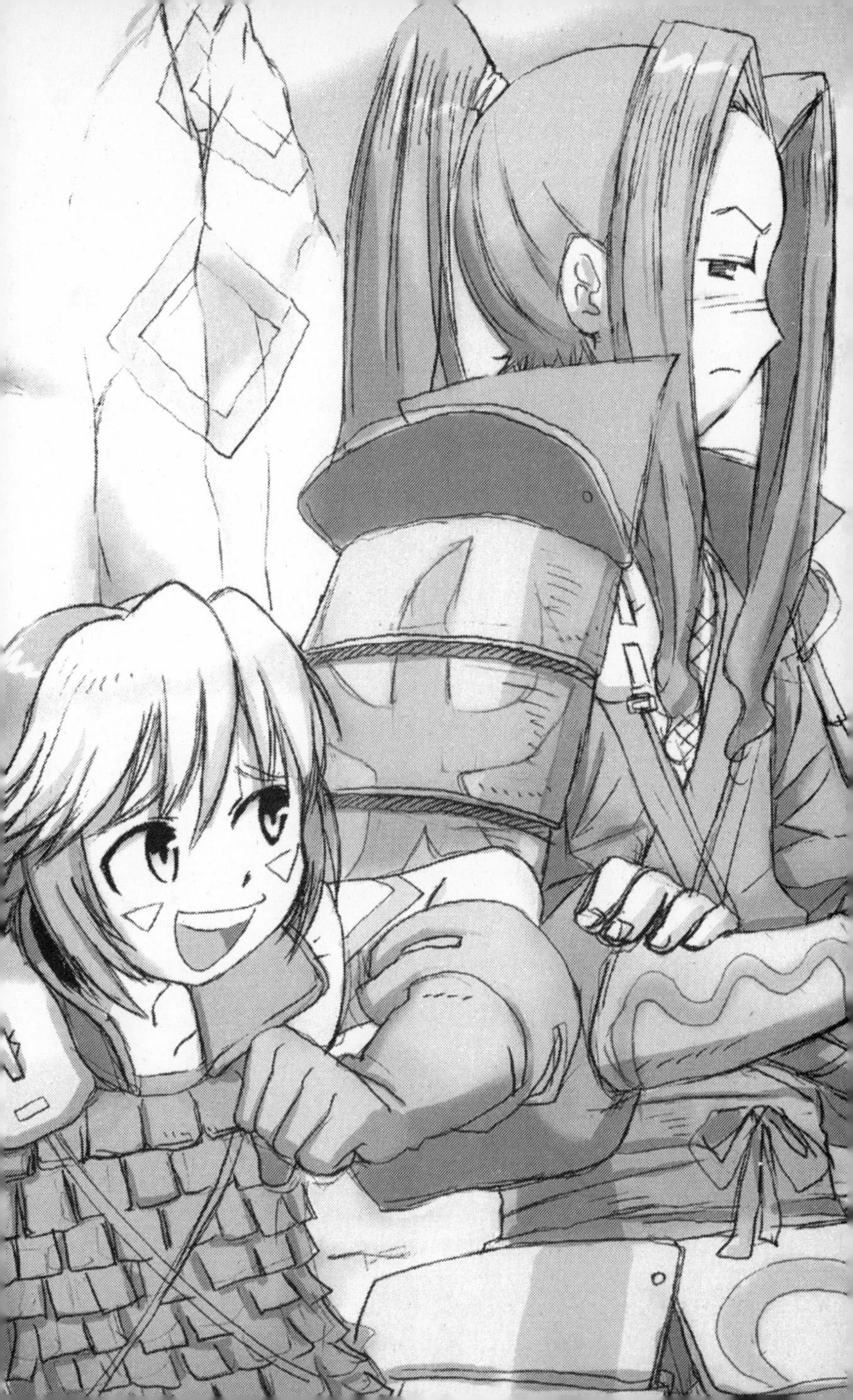

"Sure," I answered cheerfully.

"We should get going."

Chimney hurried Nova along. I waved as they warped out.

"You have new mail" flashed in the upper right corner of my display.

That was fast, I thought. *Almost too fast.*

I was about to log out so I could read it, when Kite warped in. I couldn't just disappear without at least saying something.

"Did you see the thread on the *Epitaph?* I tried e-mailing 0I directly. I'm waiting for a reply."

"I wonder if you'll get one."

"I think I already have." I smiled at Kite. "Sorry, I just got something and I want to see what it is. I'll talk to you later, okay?"

"Okay."

I logged out and checked my inbox. The message read:

```
Nyaaa! The other day rocked. This is
Mistralll. ^_^ Thanks for a fun adventure
every single time I run into you guys. So
```

y'know, I play with Kite because it's fun,
but what about you, BlackRose? It doesn't
seem like you're having much fun. Why're
you with Kite? Heh, there, I asked it! ^^;

I froze. *Should I reply? How should I answer? If I give her the
slip, will Mistral dig even deeper? Or will she let it slide?*

While I pondered this, another message from
Mistral arrived.

Ah, okay, okay . . . Maybe I should just
say this—I guess I was worried about you.
I know this is an online game and I'm just
being nosy, but I had to know, so I sent
that e-mail.

Mistral's tone had changed. It was more sisterly than when
she was playing the game. While I wrestled with my response,
yet another e-mail from Mistral arrived.

I suppose it's courteous to talk
about oneself first. ^_^; Actually, I'm a
housewife. I enjoy the game while avoiding

housework. But from my point of view, you seem like you're carrying a heavy burden. Kite has a different vibe. Kite's more open, so I can just come out and ask him. But you're more closed. It's like you're trying too hard on your own, and you're about to be crushed. So hey, if you're willing to think of me as a big sister, I'll listen to anything you have to say.

For a second, I was stunned. *Mistral's a housewife?! Mistral?*

Clearly she had picked up on my mood better than Kite ever had. *But do I dare tell her?*

I started typing.

Do I really seem like I'm at my limit? Is it really that obvious? Um—I'm a high school freshman.

Mistral replied with the suggestion that we meet.

• ⬢ •

I arrived in Dun Loireag. It was where I'd first met Mistral.

She came with her usual cheerfulness. "Been waiting long?"

"No."

"Hey, maybe we should form a party so we can talk privately."

As I accepted her invitation, I wondered what she was doing online so late. "Are you sure you're not too busy?" I asked. "I mean, what about your husband?"

Mistral laughed. "My husband gets home late. Don't worry about it."

She looked around and then suggested, "We might be spotted by someone we know, so I'll take you somewhere else. Someplace with a superb view."

"A view?"

"Yup yup. This waaaay."

I followed her. We ended up behind the alchemist shop, overlooking a valley. No one was around.

"Nice secret spot, huh? Now, sit down, sit down." Mistral folded her legs and sat.

I nervously sat next to her, wondering what she wanted to talk about.

"Now tell me—what's wrong, troubled high school girl?" she asked.

I looked at the scenery spread out below me and kept silent. Now that it was time to talk, the words wouldn't come.

Mistral filled the silence with her own thoughts. "Even though I was surprised by Kite's story, I believed him. I'll believe whatever you want to tell me, too."

Another long silence followed. Finally, I spoke, "It's about the comas. My little brother . . ."

But I couldn't continue.

"Does Kite know?" Mistral asked after a while.

"No."

"Were you playing this game with your brother?"

"No. I never played before that happened."

"I sense you're very driven, so I'm guessing you started playing to discover the cause, right?"

"Y-You're very intuitive."

"Let's just say I've known all kinds of people and listened to all kinds of problems." Mistral broke into a grin. "I hope he wakes up soon," she continued. "I'll help you, too!"

"But . . ." I trailed off.

"Hey, the phone's ringing. Hold on a minute." Mistral stopped moving. I stared at her immobile form. Suddenly, it jumped to life when she returned. "My husband has to work another shift, so we can talk all night if you want."

"Um—"

"Oh, don't worry. We don't have to be serious. But if you want, we can talk about anything. After all, why not rent Mistral for an evening of chat?"

I chuckled.

"You finally laughed!"

Mistral and I ended up talking for hours. I told her about my brother, how my family had changed, the bullying in my tennis club, Risa, everything. But the only thing I couldn't say was why Fumikazu was in a coma. I couldn't bring myself to tell her it was my fault.

● ◆ ●

My cell started vibrating as I walked to practice. I glanced down at it with surprise.

It was a text message from Asaoka.

My cold has finally gotten better. I bet practice hasn't been the same without me, right? ^_^; I'll be back starting today, so I'll see you later.

P.S. This time I'll make it to the finals!

I smiled as I continued to the clubhouse. As usual, I was early, so I entered the deserted building and headed for the lockers. I started changing when I heard someone enter.

"Hayami, you here?" Natori peeked around the locker as I finished getting into my uniform.

"Yes."

"Good. I wanted to talk to you. Is now a good time?"

"Uh, sure."

She bowed. "I'm sorry about the other day."

She lifted her head and smiled. It felt as if time melted away.

When I first joined the tennis club, Natori had helped me out and taught me a lot. We used to be friends.

"Eventually, I'll win back my spot as first string!" she said semi-jokingly.

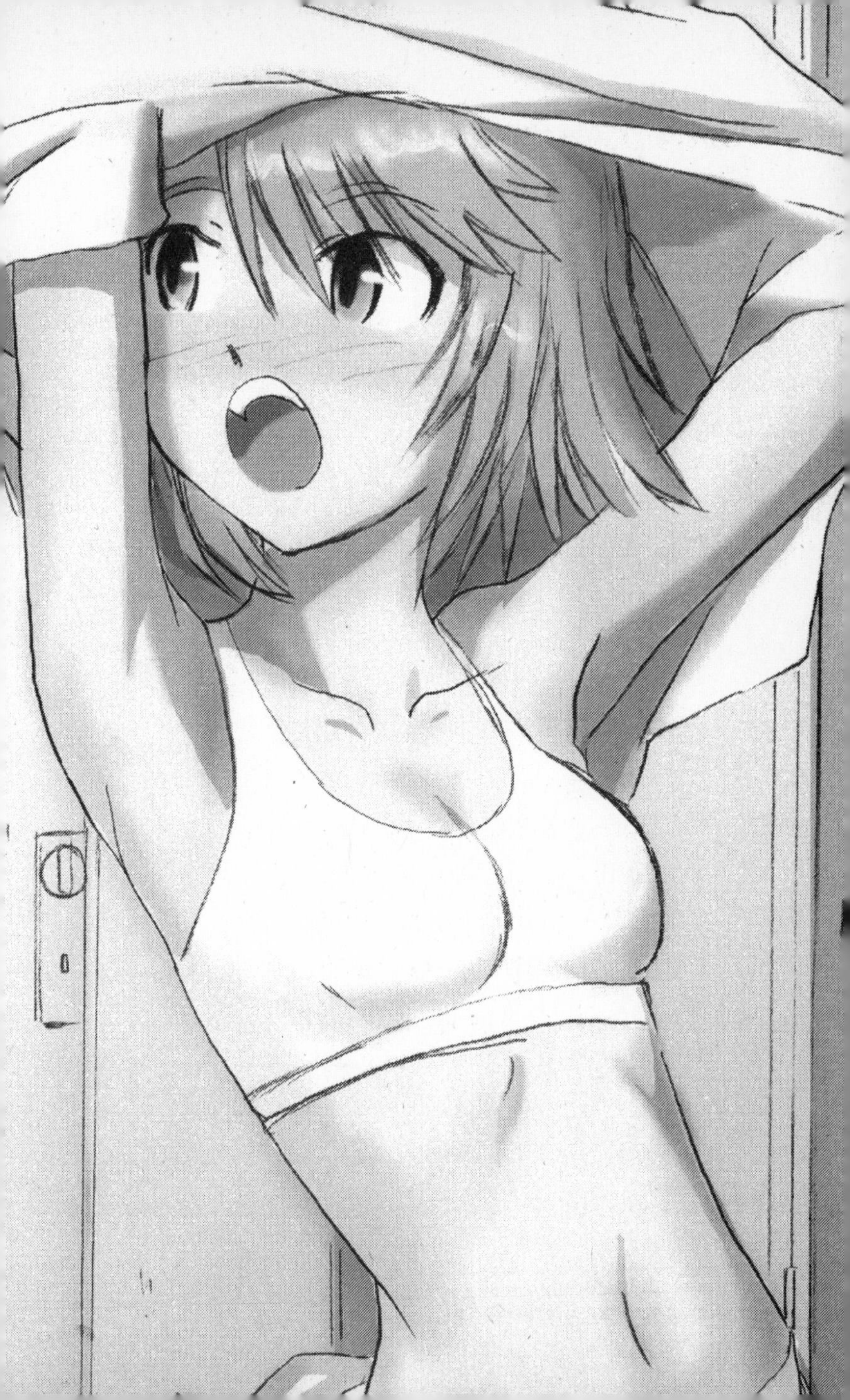

"Not from me, you won't!" It felt good to be friends again.

Suddenly, she burst into laughter.

"What's so funny?"

"It just feels refreshing," she said. I knew exactly what she meant.

We headed for the courts together. The sight of us surprised some of the others who were already there. A few minutes later, I saw Asaoka. She waved.

Practice was short because the sun set earlier these days, but it was the best practice I'd had in a long time. Afterward, Risa came up to me while I was locking up the equipment room.

"Hey! What happened?" she asked.

"What do you mean?"

"Don't give me that. You were getting along with Natori."

"Things are back to normal, that's all," I said, smiling. Risa wasn't satisfied. "Just like that?"

"Yeah. Just like that. She apologized. It was nice."

"Good. I'm glad you finally told me something. But it would be nice if I didn't always have to pry information out of you. You could, you know, just tell me sometimes."

"I know . . ." I was carrying too much of a burden. I remembered Mistral's advice about letting friends help out. I realized I wasn't alone. I had lots of friends.

"I do rely on you, you know," I said jokingly.

"Oh really? Like when?"

"Like when I need help with my homework."

Asaoka's voice called us from the clubroom.

"Race you there!" Risa challenged.

"Winner gets treated to a meat bun!"

"You're more into food than boys, Hayami."

"Are we on?"

"You bet. Let's go!" Risa took off running.

In a flash I overtook her. But as we ran, I noticed my shoelaces were untied.

"Take your time, Hayami!" Risa shouted as she passed me.

We both arrived at the doorway where Asaoka waited. We greeted her and Risa left to change.

Once we alone, Asaoka bowed. "I'm sorry to worry you," she said.

"Worry me. About what? I'm fine. If anything, I should thank you."

"Thank me?"

"For telling me about the *Epitaph of Twilight*. It really bailed me out."

She looked at me questioningly. I decided to tell her about what happened in The World. She listened quietly.

"So there's some mysterious link between that game and the *Epitaph of Twilight*. Interesting." Asaoka paused. "I might have to give The World a try," she continued.

I felt nervous. I didn't want Asaoka jumping into the game when it was so dangerous.

"Of course, I won't have time to play anything until exams are over."

"Right!" I exclaimed. "Failing because of a game would be silly."

Asaoka grinned. "I'll try researching a little on my own. I'll let you know if I find anything good," she offered.

"Thanks."

• ⬡ •

I came to Λ: Formless, His, Footprints to check on someone. The odd thing was, I didn't even know the person

fellow

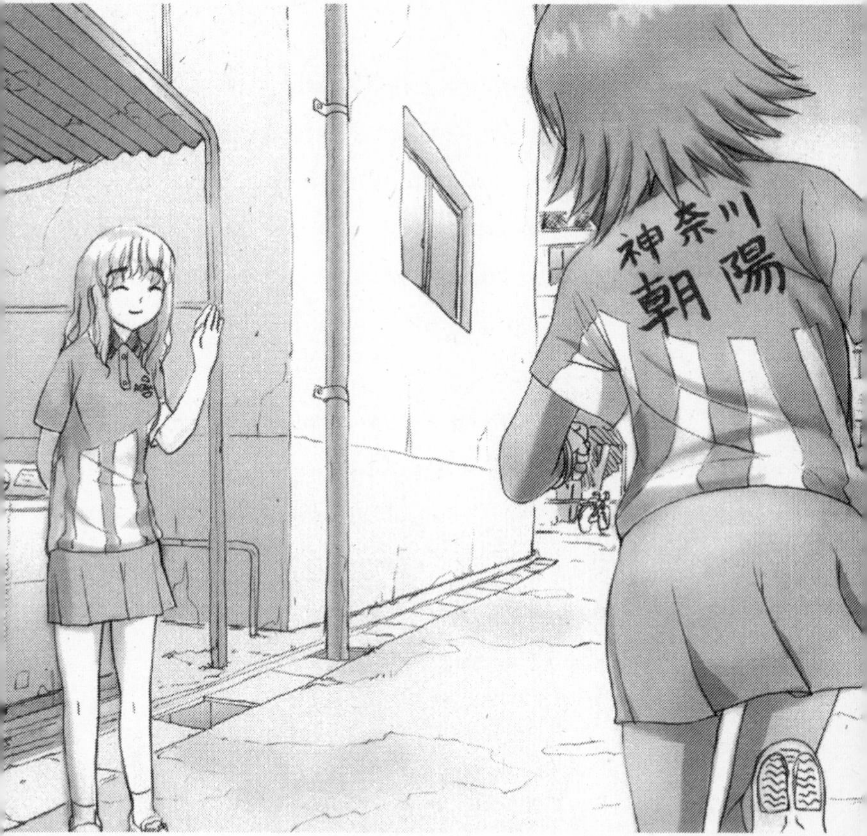

神奈川
朝陽

I was looking for. I was about to enter a field to level up against enemies when someone called out to me. "Um, please excuse me!"

I turned around to see a tall female Heavy Axeman and a heroic-looking Blademaster. Then, appearing from between the two, stepped a short Wavemaster.

"Sorry for bothering you! Are you alone?" The Wavemaster's childlike voice reminded me of Mistral. "My name is Coo," she said. "This is Kira and Nei. Did we surprise you? I'm sorry."

"No, you just remind me of someone I know." I laughed. Because parties can only be made up of three people, they couldn't have been asking for my help.

"We have a favor to ask," said Nei. She was tall and slender, with long gray hair.

A favor?

"Can you help? At least hear us out," said Kira, the Blademaster.

He was clad in pale silver armor and helmet. He had the same hairstyle as Kazu. I wondered if he had modeled his character on what he really looked like. I suddenly remembered Kazu happily talking about his own character.

"What kind of favor?" I asked.

"Well, hmm, how should I put this . . ."

Nei poked Kira. "Nobody's going to listen to you if you ask like that!"

"Just tell her the story," added Coo.

The two women seemed to pick on him mercilessly.

"Okay, there's this PC, and we think she's in trouble—" Kira continued.

"We *know* she's in trouble," Nei jumped in.

"Right, we know she is. If she's still alive—"

"She won't be, if you keep dragging this out," Coo interrupted. "Oh, let me tell it."

Coo explained that they were crossing a field to return to town when they witnessed a PC being chased by a monster. They had been too wounded to come to her aid, so they watched helplessly as she took refuge in the dungeon.

"If you don't have any particular plans, we thought maybe you could see if she's okay," Coo concluded.

I agreed to look for her while I was adventuring, and we exchanged member addresses because they wanted to know the outcome.

I warped in.

It was a very high-level area, suitable for 39 and up. Perfect for me, but definitely too high for the group I'd just encountered.

I stood in a meadow. Yellow magic portals were scattered randomly across the field. I took off running with my large sword at the ready.

Several portals opened as I ran past, but I quickly cut down the monsters that emerged. Finally, I arrived at the large dragon's opened mouth, which served as the entrance to the dungeon. Inside, it resembled a dank cave. As soon as I entered, I heard someone behind me.

I turned and saw a figure moving in the darkness. I recognized Kira's description of the avatar.

"She's a short Blademaster with dark brown hair in twin tails," he'd told me. It was one of the few times Coo had let him talk.

"It's okay; I'm not going to hurt you."

The PC stepped out of the darkness. She was clad in pale blue armor. She held an immense sword that was disproportionately large compared to her body.

I recognized her. This was the PC I'd read about in Fumikazu's journal.

"Are you Haru?" I asked.

"Huh? Have we met?"

"No. But several PCs saw you running. They asked me to check on you."

Haru grabbed my arm and asked, "Was it Kazu?!"

She knew my brother! It made my heart ache. I shook my head.

"I'm sorry they bothered you." She bowed. "I'm sure you have better things to do than check on some stranger."

"I don't mind," I replied.

I wanted to ask her about Kazu. But I didn't know how to broach the subject.

"Shall we head back?" I inquired.

"I can't," she said. "There's something I have to get. It's in this dungeon."

"Okay, I'll help you!"

Haru looked at me. She seemed suspicious of my intentions. I understood.

"I'll go for the experience while you go for the Gott Statue. Our goals are different, but our destination's the same. Let's go!"

The smile returned to her face. "Right!" she cried.

I felt like a knight protecting a princess as I crushed monster after monster on our downward journey. Finally, we reached the lowest level and arrived in the Gott Statue room. Haru slowly approached the treasure chest. Once it was open, she didn't say anything. Finally, she muttered, "This isn't it."

"What were you looking for?" I asked.

She handed me the treasure, a simple infantry cap, as a gift.

"You promise you won't make fun?" she asked.

"I promise."

"I have a friend that I haven't seen in a long time. We used to play together all the time, but lately he hasn't logged in."

I knew she was talking about my brother.

"Anyway, whenever he comes back, I wanted to surprise him with a gift. I know he was looking for a powerful wand, and I heard it was in this dungeon. But I guess whoever posted it on the BBS lied." She paused. "I just wish I knew what happened to him. He doesn't even respond to my e-mails. It's just not like him."

I was surprised to learn that there were others, besides me and my family, waiting for Fumikazu to return.

Haru suddenly felt embarrassed. "I'm sorry, I shouldn't be complaining to a stranger like this, especially after I wasted your time when you helped me get down here."

"It wasn't a waste. I'm glad I got to hear your story."

"Really?"

"Yeah. Tell me more about him."

"Kazu? He's so nice! He helped me out just like you did today. We've gone on tons of adventures; he's always been so friendly. Not just in the game either. Sometimes we talk about real life. Have you ever met anyone like that in the game?"

I thought of Mistral. "Yes, I have. It's nice to meet good people, isn't it?"

"Sure is."

She fell silent.

"What?" I asked.

"I was just thinking about your voice, BlackRose."

"What about it?"

"It kinda sounds a little like Kazu."

"Really?"

"Yeah, the way you talk is kind of similar," she added excitedly.

"I feel complimented to be compared to someone so noble. Anyway, we should get back to town."

"Okay." She used Sprite Ocarina to immediately warp from the dungeon and return to the Chaos Gate. I had to do the same if I was going to keep up. She was waiting for me when I arrived.

"I really can't thank you enough for helping me today," she said.

"Don't sweat it. Just don't get in over your head anymore."

"Will we meet again?" she asked.

"Of course!"

Haru smiled and logged out.

I was going to see Fumikazu tomorrow, and I couldn't wait to tell him about what happened today. Of course, I wouldn't mention that Haru was searching for his wand. I'd let her surprise him whenever he regained consciousness.

● ◆ ●

Kite forwarded me an e-mail from Linda, the woman who knew of Orca's search in The World. She wrote that Balmung seemed to be retracing Orca's footsteps. Kite added his own note explaining that he planned to do the same.

I had to join him. I logged in and waited at the Chaos Gate for Kite to appear. It took awhile, but when he finally showed, he didn't seem surprised to see me.

"Where to?" I asked.

"This time it's Λ: Dying, Madness, Haunted Land. It's another protected area."

"Okay, let's get going!"

I stood beside Kite as he inserted virus cores into the cross that opened up. Once the cores were in place, the protection was broken.

Λ: Dying, Madness, Haunted Land was a jungle. Even the path to the dungeon was a labyrinth that eventually led to ruins. It was this area's dungeon.

We carefully checked out every room until we arrived at the end.

"Is this the last one?" I asked.

Kite entered without answering me. I hurried after him. As soon as we entered the room, the display went dark. I thought the computer might be loading data, but it was taking too long. I felt uneasy.

The dark display switched to a dazzling brightness. Once my eyes adjusted, my breath caught when I saw the scene before us.

Suspended from a ceiling that seemed to stretch on forever was a single empty birdcage. Scattered on the ground were various broken and rusted birdcages lying in ruin.

This place had the same atmosphere as the room with the blank-eyed teddy bears.

A voice echoed around us: "When the finger points to yonder moon, the fool will not look at the fingertip."

"I think it's a fragment of the *Epitaph*," Kite whispered.

Suddenly, someone warped in next to me. It was Balmung.

"You again. Why are *you* here?!"

He glared at me, then turned to Kite.

"I don't have time to quarrel with you at present." Kite stood his ground. "I want you to tell me what's lurking through The World," he said, referring to something Linda had told us.

Balmung had to know about it, especially since he'd been working with Orca. But he refused to answer. "It has nothing to do with you."

"Yes, it does!" Kite insisted.

I realized that Balmung was acting just like I used to. I kept everything to myself because I wanted to be tough.

He thinks he has to do all this himself. But he's wrong.

"Balmung of the Azure Sky—Orca of the Azure Sea—shouldn't your goals be the same? Isn't there some connection between what's wrong here and the girl Aura?" asked Kite.

Balmung shook his head. "I won't let you cause any more damage. Listen to me! Don't interfere!"

Before we could say another word, he warped out.

"He's pigheaded too!" I said in frustration. But I wondered how he'd gotten into a protected area.

Maybe he followed us?

We headed back and logged out. Shortly after disbanding, I had an e-mail from 0I. I quickly read it and forwarded it to Kite.

Kite, here's the reply I got from 0I:

I posted everything I know about the *Epitaph of Twilight*. I do not know anything beyond that. But I got my information from a PC named Wiseman. You might be able to ask him for more details. However, he's very stubborn, so instead of me playing the middleman, it might be best if you talked to him directly. He's often in Λ: Dazzling, Sage's, Arctic.

I say we meet with Wiseman. We need to figure out our next step, right?

As soon as I sent the message, another one arrived. This one was from Lios. I didn't want to open it, but I knew I had to.

Subject: standby orders.

Thanks to your activities, our workload has doubled. We can't afford any more problems, so I'm ordering you both to stand down. Do not continue your investigation. Even if you encounter another irregular, take no action.

I deleted the message.

What the hell is his problem? Who cares about his workload? We're trying to save lives!

Lios' message only reaffirmed my decision to no longer listen to his orders. I didn't care how much he complained about the work we were causing—we needed to continue investigating. We needed to solve the riddle.

He Showed Us the Way

I had another rendezvous with Kite in Carmina Gadelica. As usual, I arrived early.

Before logging on, Mistral and I had instant messaged each other. I updated her on my life, but we also talked about silly things like the new songs from pop sensations and which celebrities we thought were cute; in other words, girl talk. I was sure this was her way of keeping me distracted so I wouldn't worry all the time. It was very sweet of her.

At one point, I asked how well she knew Kite. Mistral said she also exchanged e-mails with him, but they didn't talk the way she and I did, so she didn't know very much about his real life. Or maybe she just told me that to protect his privacy.

Finally, Kite arrived. "Waiting long?" he asked.

"Nah. I got here early." He was late, but I wasn't going to say anything . . . though I wondered what had kept him. *Is he late because of homework, or is he held up by his job?* I still knew so little about him.

It was considered rude to ask people about their real life while playing the game. I remember Kazu lecturing me about this in front of the PC. At the same time, we'd done so much together in The World that I felt as if I did ask Kite about his personal life, he would tell me.

But I didn't. I was afraid if I asked him about his life, he might ask me about mine. And I still wasn't ready to open up to him.

We warped to Λ: Dazzling, Sage's, Arctic. It wasn't protected.

• ⬡ •

Powdery snow fell as far as the eye could see. The barren landscape was devoid of any characters.

"Maybe he's in the dungeon?" Kite mused.

"Well, 0I only said he was in the area—he didn't say *where* in the area he might be."

"Yeah, I couldn't imagine him having much fun just standing out here," Kite joked.

We headed for the dungeon. The entrance wasn't very far, and we quickly explored every corner of its castle-like maze. Once we finished searching, we retraced our steps, but the place was empty.

It was possible that if he were wandering around, we could always be in one area while he was in another, or he might not be here at all. I started to wish 01 had given us more information. Either way, I couldn't figure out why Wiseman would hang out in this desolate place anyway.

Is he eccentric?

When we returned to the lowest level, I said, "What if he's not here at all, and he's actually in the field?"

"Then I give up." Kite laughed.

We entered a remarkably large chamber and caught sight of three other PCs. There were two Blademasters and a tall white-haired Wavemaster wearing a jet-black coat that stretched to the floor.

One of these guys could be Wiseman . . .

Kite and I slowly approached the trio. As we neared, the two Blademasters thanked the Wavemaster and warped out. The Wavemaster heard us approaching and turned. His skin was dark, and he had a strange symbol etched on his forehead.

"Did you come to trade?" he asked in a calm, deep voice.

I placed the cursor over him to learn his name. It was Wiseman.

"Um . . . we'd like to ask you about the *Epitaph of Twilight.*" Kite spoke nervously.

"*Epitaph of Twilight?*" Wiseman spoke slowly, as if tasting each word in his mouth. "Such knowledge comes at a steep price."

"Price?" I echoed.

"What are your terms?" Kite asked.

"Give me time. I'll let you know my offer via e-mail."

"All right." Kite nodded.

"If we have to wait, then that should lower the price," I snapped. I figured if we were conducting business, then I should haggle. *Isn't that what negotiating is about?*

Wiseman laughed.

"Very well, I will." I winked at Kite, and we left the dungeon. "I wonder what he'll ask for," I said as we exited the castle. "I haven't a clue, but it's our only lead."

Kite's voice sounded weary as he answered, "Looks like it."

He said he was off for the day, and he logged out. I wondered if he was feeling sick or something, but since I couldn't do anything about his problems in the real world, I decided I'd help Kite out in The World.

I wonder why saying goodbye to him made me feel so forlorn . . . I wanted to chat with Mistral again, so I e-mailed her and talked about Fumikazu. In many ways, I felt like she was BlackRose's older sister. Mistral's response came surprisingly fast. She said not to hold back, and that she'd help me figure out the *Epitaph of Twilight.*

I thanked her and got ready for bed.

● ⬡ ●

I rummaged around the music storage room looking for a mix tape I'd recorded the previous year. It was for a dance class.

I could hear the band practicing in the music room next door. The trombonist had trouble staying in tune.

I nearly jumped when a voice behind me asked, "What're you doing?"

I turned to see one of the band members standing in the doorway. He had pale skin, dyed caramel-colored hair, and thin eyebrows.

"I'm looking for a tape," I answered.

"If it's not on those shelves, it's probably in one of these boxes." He pointed next to the shelves beside me.

"Thanks," I muttered, returning to my task. I could still feel his eyes on me. I crouched and opened one of the boxes he'd pointed at. It wasn't long before I found the tape.

"Here it is!" I held it up triumphantly.

"Good for you." He smiled, walking toward me.

I didn't realize how big he was. *How come I never noticed him before? Is he an upperclassman?*

He brushed against me as he walked past. I was sort of trapped in the corner. He opened another box, removed a pair of drumsticks, and smiled.

"Excuse me, I'm in your way." I tried to leave, but found I couldn't.

"You're Hayami, right? A freshman?"

"Yes."

"I can see the tennis courts from right here. I've watched you practice."

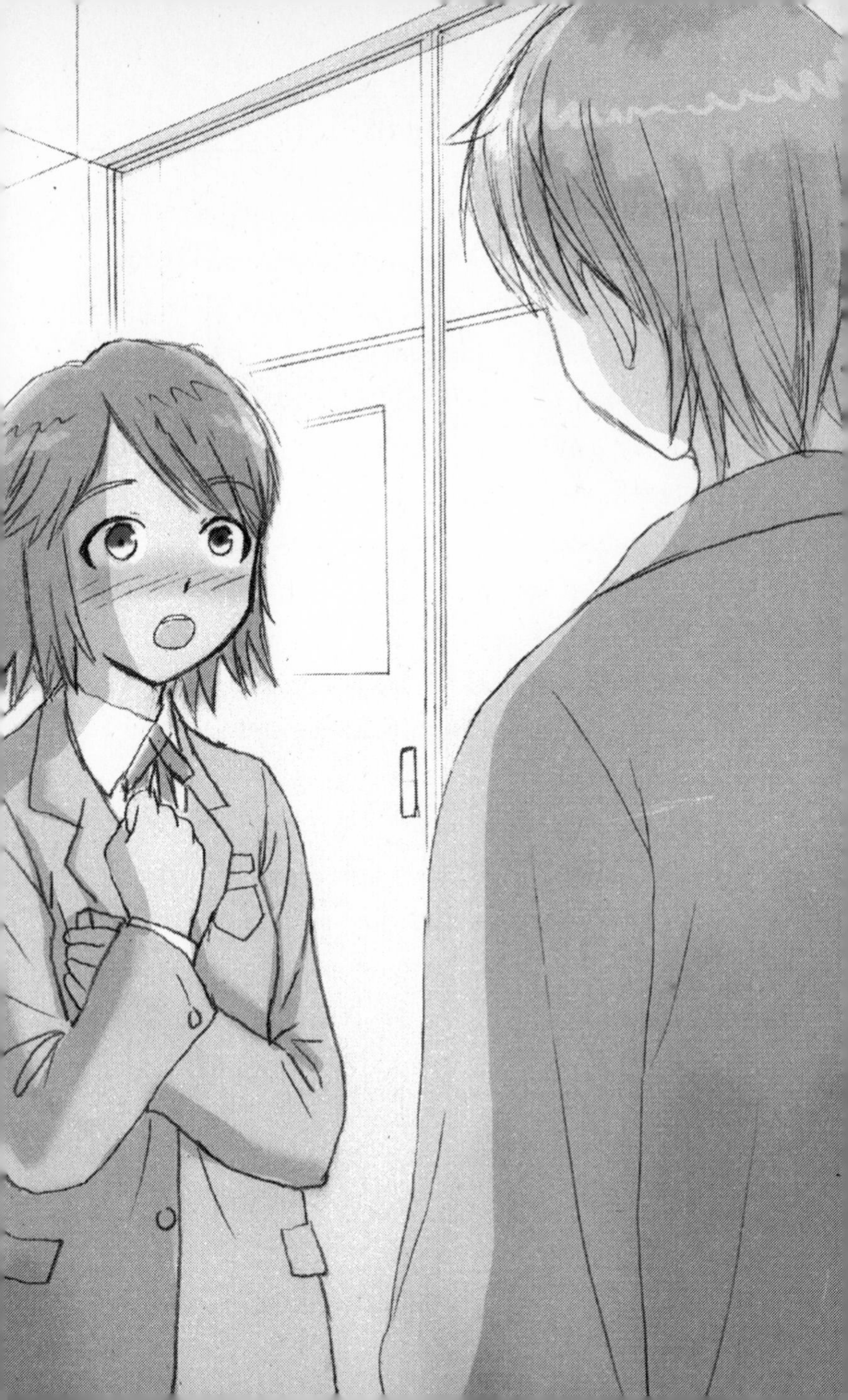

I was bewildered.

"Sorry. I'm normally not so direct, but I've never run into you before." He peered at my face. "I watched you struggle. It made me admire you."

My face went red. *How long has he been watching me?*

"It looks like you're getting along better with your teammates now."

He even knew I was being bullied? Is this guy a stalker?

"Uh, don't get me wrong. I'm not a stalker or anything," he said, as if reading my mind. Suddenly, his face turned beet red. Looking anywhere but at me, he asked, "Would you like to go out with me?"

"Hey! You got those sticks or what?" a voice called from the music room.

"I'll be right there!" he shouted back.

He quickly grabbed a pen and looked for something to write on. Finding an old music score, he muttered, "I guess this'll work," then scribbled his number and handed me the paper.

"Take it," he urged.

I stared blankly, unable to move. He gently took my hand and put the paper in it. Smiling, he turned and left.

"Akira?" The door on the other side of the room opened and Shouko entered. "Hey, are you okay?"

She must notice that I'm blushing.

Shouko saw the dust-covered tape in my hand and smiled. "I'm glad you found it. Let's get out of here."

I looked at the paper the upperclassman had handed me. On it were his name, cell phone number, and e-mail address.

"What's that?" Shouko asked.

"Nothing."

We quickly left the room. Once we were in the hall, I told Shouko everything that happened.

"He's pretty sly." Shouko grinned and poked me in the arm.

"He's just messing with me," I muttered.

"I don't think so," she said, and looked at the paper he'd handed me. "What's his name?"

I looked at the paper. His handwriting was terrible.

"Hagiya," I answered.

"Oh, I think I know him. He's a junior. Do you remember he played in the band at the freshman welcome party?"

"He did?"

"Yuuji admired his playing so much, he wanted to take up guitar."

"Oh," I mumbled, and looked out the window. Right now, I didn't have time for this. I had too many other worries: Fumikazu, Kite, and the mysteries of The World. Yet despite those worries, I couldn't help feeling a little giddy being asked out.

"Are you gonna call him?" Shouko asked.

"I don't know," I answered. "I'll think about it."

As I left school, I saw him waving goodbye from the music room. I was so embarrassed that I hurried down the sidewalk without waving back.

When I came home, I found Kouta waiting for me in the hall. He was half-naked.

"Big Sis!" he shouted. "Mom says we should take a bath!"

He squealed as I picked him up and carried him into the bathroom.

While I scrubbed him down, he asked, "Did you have a good day today?"

"Yeah. Why?"

"I dunno. You just seem happy."

I changed the subject, but while he soaked in the tub and told me about his adventures in making shapes out of clay, I found myself preoccupied as I washed up. I was thinking about Hagiya.

When I returned to my room, I took out the slip of paper with his number. I decided to call him.

My heart started pounding. *Why am I so nervous? Maybe I should e-mail him instead. In some ways it will be easier. No,* I thought. *I should just call.*

I took a deep breath and punched in his number. Before it could ring, I hung up.

"This is stupid," I muttered. "Okay, let's do this." I hit redial. It started ringing before I could change my mind. I was committed.

As it rang, I suddenly found myself hoping it would go to voice mail.

"Hello."

Damn!

"Uh . . . this is Hayami." My voice was shaking.

"Oh, good. You called. I'm glad you did, though I'm not really good on the phone."

We then sat in an awkward silence. Finally, I blurted out, "Fine, I'll just do this over e-mail."

"No, no, I want to talk. I just . . . anyway, I'm sorry about today.

"Sorry?"

"About rushing this. I just didn't know when I might see you again," his voice faltered at the end. Another silence followed.

I could hear the clock on the wall ticking. Slowly, I started to calm down. I thought of myself as BlackRose. It helped . . . a little.

"Well . . . um," my voice cracked.

"Yeah?" he said, urging me on.

"Uh, I can't really do this right now." Even though he couldn't see me, I bowed my head.

After a pause, he murmured, "Oh?"

"I really am sorry."

"Don't apologize."

"I'm sorry."

"You said it again." Hagiya laughed sadly.

"Yeah. Sorry." I laughed nervously.

"Is it because you're so busy?"

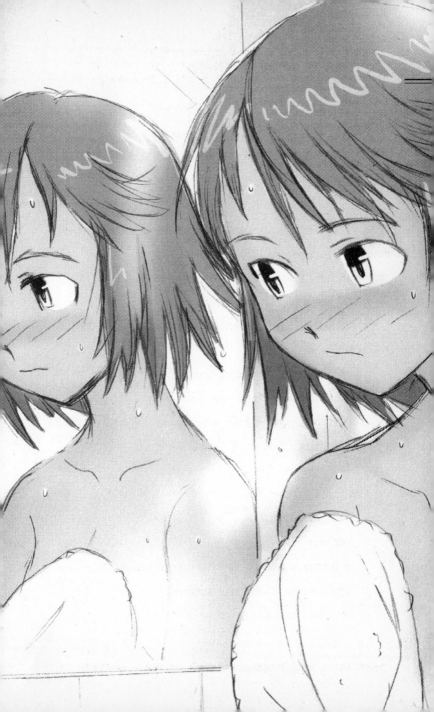

"Kinda."

"Okay. Well, I'll wait."

"Hagiya, you don't need to wait for me. I'm sure there are others who would—"

"I don't want to date any others. I want to date *you.*"

I couldn't believe he spoke so bluntly about such a thing. My cheeks felt hot.

He cleared his throat. "Sorry, I hope that doesn't sound overbearing. I'm really not."

"Oh." *What is it about me he likes?* I wondered.

"Maybe you should think about it," he said. "No harm in just thinking about it, right?"

"Um . . ."

"Okay, next time e-mail me. Maybe it'll be easier than talking."

"Huh?!"

"I'm glad you called. Even if you did turn me down. But I won't give up easily," Hagiya insisted. "Think about it and e-mail me later. Goodbye!"

He hung up. I looked at my cell phone and sighed. I clicked it shut and peered down at the paper with his information. I knew the timing just wasn't right.

I crumpled it up and tossed it in the trash.

• ⬡ •

Subject: Terms of Exchange

Let's dispense with formalities and get right to the point. The Spark Sword is supposed to be somewhere in Λ: Blooming, Promised, Walkway. If you can find the Spark Sword, I'll tell you what you need to know.

It sounded like a cheap price.

I quickly wrote to Kite and then Mistral. Once I finished, I threw on the goggles, or FMD as everyone kept correcting me, and entered The World.

Lo and behold, Kite was waiting for me beside the Chaos Gate in Carmina Gadelica. "BlackRose!" he called.

"Hey! I just wrote you."

"I know. I was waiting for you," he said.

I got a warm fuzzy feeling when he said that. Even though I'd completely forgotten about it, at that moment, something reminded me of Hagiya. But instead of dwelling on that, I said, "Sorry for making you wait."

"It's okay. I just felt like waiting for you." He chuckled a bit. "You got Wiseman's message?"

"Yeah. I knew you'd probably log on as soon as you saw it, so . . ."

"You ready to go?" Kite asked.

"You bet. Can we call Mistral?"

Kite paused. Finally, he asked, "Why Mistral?"

"I told her about Wiseman and she already knows about the *Epitaph.*"

"Okay."

We sent her an e-mail and waited for her to show. It didn't take long.

"Hope I didn't keep you two waiting."

"Not at all. Happy to see you," I said.

"Where to?" Mistral asked.

"Λ: Blooming, Promised, Walkway."

"Kinda sounds like a fairy tale." Mistral grinned.

For some reason, I expected Λ: Blooming, Promised, Walkway to be a normal area. It wasn't. The protected area menu popped up.

"Do you have enough virus cores?" I asked Kite.

"Yeah." Kite placed the cores in the open gaps.

I wondered if Wiseman knew this area was protected. If so, he sent us here thinking that we couldn't get through. *In which case, he never had any intention of giving us information on the* Epitaph of Twilight!

When we arrived, Mistral cried out, "The poor meadow's ruined!"

Originally this was a beautiful prairie, stretching beneath a deep blue sky. Now it was torn apart by black fissures and red character strings.

"Let's find the dungeon!" I said.

By the time we reached it, we'd hit several magic portals and been attacked. "This is a tough level!" I cried.

We were two or three character levels below the recommended number, but Mistral was always ready with recovery magic.

She made sure to stay behind us to avoid being hit herself.

I'm glad we called her, I thought with relief.

The monsters were so difficult that by the time we arrived at the dungeon, all three of us had gone up a level.

"Hold on a sec," Mistral called. "I need to regenerate SP."

We took a break. SP slowly regenerated with time. She'd consumed a lot of magic just keeping us alive. I checked my own item list and found plenty of Mage's Soul, an SP recovery item. I offered it to her.

"No, I have plenty of it, but I'm saving it for a boss fight. I'll be fully recovered in another minute."

"Okay."

Mistral expected the worst if she thought there'd be a boss fight. I was thinking the same. I didn't know if it would be another Data Bug or something really tough like another Skeith, but I realized her decision to preserve Mage's Souls was the right one.

"Thanks. I'm ready!" Mistral waved her wand.

We plunged forward and quickly descended to the lowest level of the old castle-like dungeon.

"I wonder where the Gott Statue's at," I said.

"It has to be around here somewhere," Mistral chimed in, and opened a nearby treasure chest. She found a recovery potion. We'd probably soon need it.

We entered a large empty chamber with only one other doorway. A purple mist hung in the air.

he_showed_us_the_way

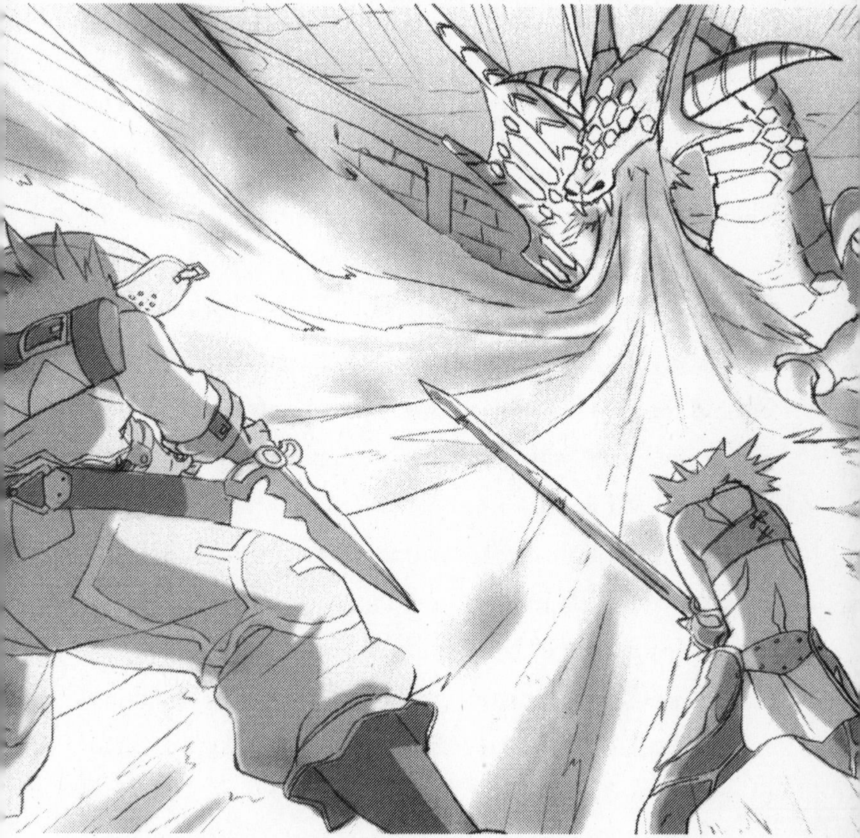

Mistral cast strengthening magic on us. Then I used Mage's Soul on Mistral.

We headed into the mist and ran right into a Data Bug. A dragon with luminescent green hexes covering its body appeared.

"Look out!" Kite warned.

We attacked.

The dragon roared and unleashed a bellow of flame at all three of us.

My HP instantly dropped to a dangerously low level. Mistral was far enough away that she wasn't affected, but Kite was nearly dead.

I opened my item list and used a recovery item on Kite. His HP jumped back to the safety zone. Mistral cast a recovery spell on me.

"It's fire-based!" Mistral called out from behind.

"Rue Kruz!" Mistral chanted, unleashing a watery attack spell. Multiple blocks of icy spikes assaulted the dragon.

The words "Elemental Hit" rose above the dragon's head. That meant it was vulnerable to the attack. Mistral had caused bonus damage.

The beast roared and shook its head in pain. We laid into it with our attacks.

Compared to Skeith or Innis, this Data Bug was weak. Only its initial flaming attack was dangerous. If you could survive that, the rest was easy.

Finally, "Protect Break OK" appeared beside the dragon. Kite fired off a data drain. The shining green hexes that coiled about the dragon scattered. The crimson dragon turned toward Kite, who was now defenseless, and charged.

Oh crap!

I quickly opened my item list and used a sleep charm. The beast fell to the ground, snoring.

"Yaaay! It's asleep!" Mistral shouted out, and cast a recovery spell on Kite.

The dragon would wake once we attacked it again, so all three of us prepared. Mistral beefed us up with strength spells and then readied her own magical attack while Kite and I stood poised, our weapons ready.

"Finish it off at once!" I shouted. All three of us simultaneously struck the dragon, killing it instantly.

"We beat it!" Mistral shouted joyfully.

"Hm," Kite mused.

"What is it?" I asked.

"I got the Spark Sword," he replied, surprised.

"So this thing had it? Yay!" Mistral carried on happily.

It seemed strange that the Data Bug should be carrying the item we were looking for. Our mission proved far easier than we'd imagined.

"I guess that's it then," Kite said.

"Let's take it to that Wiseman guy!" Mistral said.

The three of us returned to Carmina Gadelica. As Kite prepared to transition us back to the field where Wiseman hung out, I noticed Balmung talking to a merchant NPC. It had to be Lios.

"Look. It's Balmung."

I pointed, but the pair warped out before Kite saw them.

"Where?" he asked.

"Over there. He just warped out."

"Oh," Kite murmured, disappointed. I think he knew that this would be easier if we worked with Balmung.

I wondered why was Balmung talking to a System Administrator. *Is he working for Lios, too?*

When we returned to Wiseman's chamber, he seemed surprised to see us. Kite handed him the Spark Sword.

"That's definitely the Spark Sword," he verified, his voice betraying his admiration.

"You think? Now let's have that information you promised." I took a step forward.

He looked at me and asked, "Who *are* you people?"

"What's that supposed to mean?! You've got what you wanted; now give us what we want."

"I'm surprised you were able to enter a protected area." Wiseman looked at each of us as if trying to figure out which one of us managed to break the seal.

"You mean you sent us to a protected area as a *test?!*" I screamed.

"Certainly. Now I'm wondering how you managed it." He looked between me and Kite.

For whatever reason, Kite decided to tell him how and why he did it. Once Kite finished, Wiseman said, "I can't believe something like that could happen to someone as powerful as Orca of the Azure Sea."

What does he know?! I thought. *The World isn't just a game. There's something at work with some other goal.*

Then I remembered that was similiar to what Linda had said.

Wiseman said, "All right. If that's the case, I'll help you. I apologize for testing you. I'll send you what data I have on the *Epitaph of Twilight* via e-mail. And I'd also like you to have this."

Wiseman gave me the Spark Sword.

"Huh?" I was shocked.

"I don't really need it," he explained. "Besides, your story was far more interesting than any item." He smiled faintly at me and warped out.

"You did well there," Mistral said, indicating the Spark Sword.

We headed back to the town and separated. By the time I logged out of the game, Wiseman's message was already waiting. I quickly opened it.

Mutation

Unknown where the Cursed Wave
was born . . .
After the stars doth cross the
heavens,
The sky in the East doth darken
and air doth
fill with mourning.
From the chosen land beyond
the forest,
a sign of the Wave comes.
Rising the wake is Skeith,
the Shadow of Death,
to drown all that stands.
Mirage of Deceit, Innis, betrays
all with the flawed image, and
doth aid the Wave.

*And the power of Magus, a drop
from the Wave doth
reach the heavens,
and creates a new Wave.
With the Wave, Fidchell, the
power to tell the dark future:
hope darkens,
sadness and despair rule.
Gorre schemes when swallowed
by the Cursed Wave.
Macha seduces
with the sweet trap.
Wave reaches the pinnacle,
and escape none can.
Tarvos still remains
with more cruelty
to punish and destroy.
And with the turbulent
destruction, after the Wave,
only a voice remains.
And from the deep
within the void
arrives Corbenik.
Perhaps then the Wave is just
a beginning as well.*

It sounds like the monsters you encountered were the Skeith and Innis mentioned in the *Epitaph*. I recommend you get in contact with the legendary hacker Helba. Follow these directions: "East, north, south, west, north. The gate to Paradise will open." Those are the magic words to reach Net Slum. You mustn't forget them.

I pray that the weapon I gave you will prove useful.

May the Twilight Dragon's divine protection be with you both.

—Wiseman

I reread the e-mail from Wiseman over and over again.

We now had the complete list of names. There were six more enemies we had to face. But why wasn't Cubia mentioned? And did Aura have anything to do with the *Epitaph of Twilight?*

Undoubtedly so.

I wondered what Kite thought of this message. I wrote him a quick e-mail:

I guess these are the enemies we have yet to fight: Magus, Fidchell, Gorre, Macha, Tarvos, and Corbenik. But what could Net Slum be? And what are the magic words for?

• ⬡ •

I returned to Δ: Hidden, Forbidden, Holy Ground. I'd grown strong in the past two months, so if anything attacked . . . I felt I could handle it. I wanted to see Aura's statue. I wanted to see the names.

I found her statue in the deserted church, bound by chains. I peered at the pedestal, trying to see what came after Magus. Nothing else was discernible. Only the first three names: Skeith . . . Innis . . . Magus . . .

I leaned back, lost in thought. *Why are they carved into the pedestal?*

For a moment, I thought I saw the statue move. But I knew it was just my imagination.

I left the church and headed back to Mac•Anu. Suddenly I realized the faint buzzing noise that had been

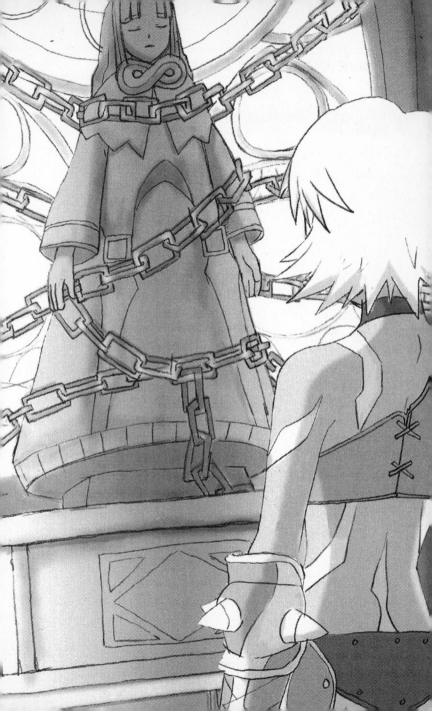

bugging me for the past few seconds wasn't part of the game, but it was my cell phone ringing. I quickly threw off my goggles to answer it, but I was too late. Caller ID told me it was Asaoka.

Why would she be calling me at this hour?

I dialed her number, but it was busy. I decided to text message her and asked her to call me back.

I lay down in bed with the cell in my hand, wondering why she'd called. I dozed off waiting for a reply.

●◆●

"Do you wanna be a ghost?" Miho asked. "They're asking for volunteers. I think it'll be fun. C'mon, let's do it." She raised her hand.

I grimaced.

Our class was creating a haunted house for the culture festival in November. I didn't really like the idea of being a spook. I never got into scary stuff like that. The supernatural made me uneasy.

Instead, I was still thinking about Asaoka's e-mail.

Hey! Did you know I'm in the same class as Hagiya? He told me you two had talked. Anyway, he's going to perform at the culture festival and he wants to play a song that you like. He asked me for your e-mail address, but I told him I couldn't give it to him without asking you first. That's why I called last night.

He was being persistent. *Didn't I already turn him down? Now he's trying to go through Asaoka.* I wondered what she might have said to him about me.

"Boo!"

I looked up at Miho.

"You space out too much, Akira," she muttered.

"She's just worn out now that meets and exams are over."

Risa poked me.

"C'mon, don't you think it'll be fun to be ghosts? They say sometimes people act differently when they're behind a mask. Sometimes the person's real desires are revealed."

"If we're ghosts, we won't be able to see the other booths." I didn't want to do it.

"Too late," Miho said. "I already volunteered us both."

Shouko leaned over and whispered, "Hey, if you wanna get out of it, you can sneak away and see the live show."

"Live show? What live show?"

"The one Hagiya's performing in."

Is this a conspiracy? Did Asaoka tell her? She must have. Don't they understand that I've already turned him down?

"No thanks," I answered bluntly.

Shouko looked at me and shrugged. "I guess this is no time for love, then."

"Love?!" I squeaked.

My heart sank over this matchmaking plot. And seeing my name added to the list under "Ghosts" didn't help any.

● ⬢ ●

There was a new post on the BBS relating to Aura. It stated that a strange character, probably a roving AI, was talking about Net Slum. He was in Δ: Scattering, Fossil's, Milestone. So Kite and I met outside the Chaos Gate and headed there.

The contamination had now managed to infiltrate an unprotected area. The snowfield was scorched red.

Areas that normal characters could reach were starting to break down. *Why doesn't Lios shut it down?*

We reached the lowest level of the dungeon and found a Wavemaster. His avatar was filled with holes; I could see through it. He was damaged, just like the area.

His name was Plaird. I wondered if he were a character from *Epitaph of Twilight.*

"Do you know? I'm looking for something. Do you know where it is?" Plaird babbled.

"What're you looking for?" Kite nervously asked.

"I don't know; that's why I'm looking. I don't know. What is 'I don't know'?"

"Come on, stop playing around," I said to Plaird.

Plaird spoke rapidly, "Come on? Come off? Rendezvous in Net Slum. Rendezvous in Λ: Pulsating, Worst, Core. Rendezvous with no schedule. I hope you can make our rendezvous. I'm sure you can make our rendezvous. What's 'rendezvous'? What's 'looking'? What's 'what'? I don't know what I don't know."

"We don't know either," I muttered. I couldn't tell what was wrong with him, but at least he gave us the keywords for Net Slum.

Through the holes in his avatar, I could see someone warp in behind him. An instant later, Plaird was deleted.

Kite·and I were too stunned for words.

Standing behind where Plaird once stood was Lios. He put his hands on his hips and said scornfully, "Just faulty data!"

"Lios! What did you *do?!*" Kite shouted.

"I debugged. That's my *job.*" Lios glared at us. "I thought I told you to stay put until further instructions. If you don't want to be deleted like your friend here, then you'd better obey my commands!" Lios warped out as quickly as he had arrived.

I couldn't believe he actually threatened to delete our characters. *Will he really do it?* Part of me believed he would.

I tried not to get angry and instead thought about Plaird's words. He said that Net Slum was located in Λ: Pulsating, Worst, Core. Kite and I agreed to go. We had to return to Carmina Gadelica first.

When we arrived, we ran into Balmung.

He and Kite stared at each other for a moment. Then Balmung said, "Use it."

A moment passed before Kite mumbled, "Thanks." But Balmung had already warped out.

I realized he'd handed Kite something. "Hey, what'd you get?" I asked.

"Hm? Oh, nothing. We should go," Kite said, avoiding my question.

"By ourselves?"

"Yeah."

"Hey! Why don't you invite *me?!*" We turned to see Mistral running toward us.

"Should we bring her?" I asked Kite in party chat.

"Why not?" he replied.

Mistral's status appeared at the bottom of the screen. She said, "Excellent. Let's have fun today!"

We faced the Chaos Gate as Kite entered the coordinates. Naturally, it was another protected area. Kite hesitated.

"You okay? Got enough virus cores?" I asked.

"Yeah. I just got that one recently, so we can go."

Which one is he talking about? Before I could ask, the screen went white, and we warped.

A prairie stretched before our eyes. There were the worm-eaten graphics typical of a protected area.

"East, north, south, west, north. The gate to Paradise will open," I mumbled the magic words written in the e-mail from Wiseman, but nothing happened. "I guess that didn't work."

Kite laughed.

"Don't laugh—think of something!"

I realized we still hadn't told Mistral about the info on the *Epitaph* from Wiseman. I explained to her the circumstances that led us to this area.

"Maybe it's some kinda route. Like in the dungeon," Mistral mused.

"That's probably it."

We soon found the dungeon, this one in the shape of an old castle. The three of us entered. The first room was a perfect square. When we tried to leave, however, we ended up right back in the same room we started in.

"Argh! I can't stand frustrating stuff like this! You deal with it!" I said.

"I think this is where we use those directions," Kite said, frowning.

"What do you mean?" I asked.

"Just go east, north, south, west, and north," Mistral said merrily, and then I caught on.

You could go one of four ways from the small square room. It was possible to choose east, west, south, and north.

"Oh, right. So that's it."

When we moved according to the magic words, a set of stairs leading down appeared.

"We figured it out!" I exclaimed.

"Now let's find Net Slum!"

We descended and found ourselves in another pure white room. The only thing inside was a rundown Shinto shrine archway. In the background was a strange sound . . . like someone speaking quickly, but too quickly to comprehend. I tried to ignore it.

"What do you think? A dead end?" Kite asked.

"It feels strange . . . We've come this far, haven't we?" I replied.

Suddenly, the screen went pitch-black and there was a horrid screech. We had warped.

We found ourselves in what looked like a bombed-out town. More than a slum, this place was in ruins. Standing around were avatars with strange faces. Some of them had emoticons for faces, another had a picture frame, a third was a fish.

"So this is Net Slum?" Kite murmured.

"Creepy. What *are* these guys?" I asked.

An avatar near the archway with a TV for a face spoke up. "We call it Paradise," she said, her tone polite.

"Where's Helba?" Kite asked.

The TV-faced avatar walked away without answering.

"I guess we just keep looking," Kite said. "Maybe talk to the people here."

We proceeded along the gloomy, narrow alley.

I felt uneasy. I wondered if the information Wiseman had given us was fake. *Why would Helba be in a place like this?* "Helba's a hacker, isn't she?"

Kite answered, "Yeah. She helped us fight Cubia . . ."

Along the way, we tried asking several characters about Helba, but none of their answers made any sense.

"I don't know, I don't know. I really don't know."

"Are you really awake right now? Our dream is very real, you see."

"I don't need light! I need water. Give me water!"

One rambled on for a long time: "The process of thinking a thing through achieves a high degree of perfection through the repetition of soliloquy. Before seeking salvation from others, you should find it for yourself. Therefore, I will not answer your question about Helba."

"This is getting us nowhere," I said. "I wonder if anyone here can hold a real conversation."

We trudged our way to the center of the ruins.

A little old man popped up before us, appearing seemingly out of nowhere.

"Are you looking for Helba?" he asked.

"Yes," Kite answered.

"I'm Tartarga," he nodded. "It so happens I heard from her recently. You want to know about the *Epitaph*, right? It's a saga that tells how the Age of the Spirits came to an end. But the texts are scattered. And when they are found, they are extremely difficult to comprehend. Yes, it's very tricky business."

"Say, uh, can you tell me why the people around here all look so strange?" I asked.

"This place was once where all of the unsuccessful non-player characters drifted. It's sort of a junkyard-turned-sanctuary for failures. Players eventually stumbled into here and found these failed characters amusing. They've since added their own variations to copy attributes of failed characters. Now the boundary between player and non-player characters is quite indistinct. Some of them simply don't know which category they fall into anymore. Only their character data remains intact as they wander the network. It's the same fate as Harald."

"Harald?" That was the name attached to the item we found in the weird room.

A strange voice suddenly echoed around us: "I must speak with Morganna. To go where she is, the living flesh poses a hindrance. But I must. I must go! For our Aura. Emma, please give me a little more courage."

I sensed something above me and when I looked, I saw Helba floating through the air.

She slowly descended from the sky and then hovered over us.

"They're the words of The World's creator, Harald Hoerwick."

The World's creator?

"So what brings you here?" Helba asked.

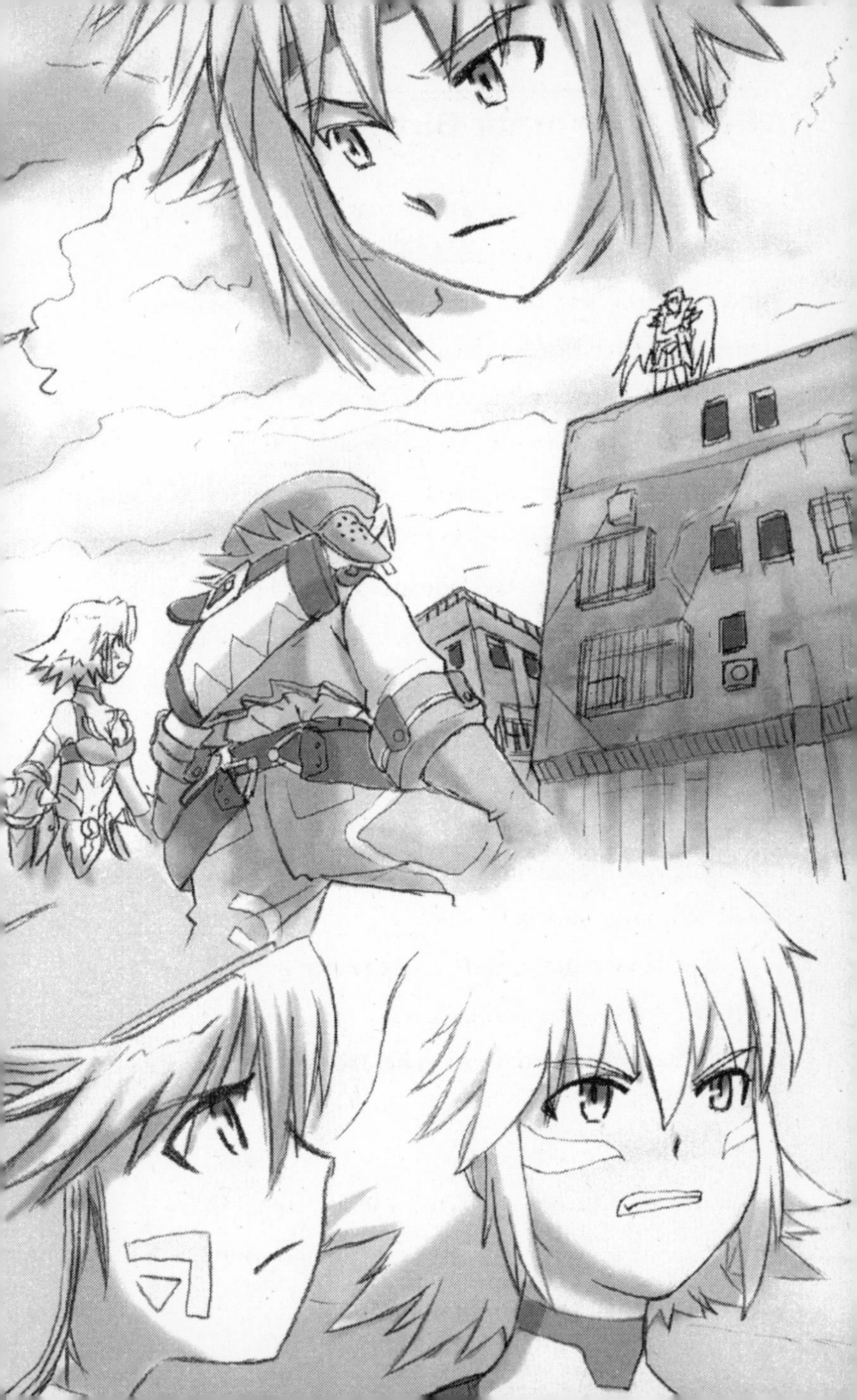

Kite told her of the series of events that led us here in our pursuit of the *Epitaph of Twilight.*

"Both of you have succeeded in reaching it as well, I see. You've done well," she said. Then, raising her head, "Oh, look. We have an unexpected guest. As a representative of Net Slum, I welcome you to Paradise!"

Turning, I saw a figure standing on a tower of ruins, his arms folded defiantly.

"Balmung!" Kite said, surprised.

"I see you sided with Lios. You cracked easily, for someone who was so sure of himself." Helba chuckled.

"Don't judge me. I'm not like you!" Balmung pointed his sword at Helba.

She continued talking, unperturbed. "Shadowing your friend is quite shameful. You've disgraced the name of the Descendant of Fianna."

I realized that Balmung must have given Kite the virus core he needed to break the protection. But because Balmung couldn't get into protected areas himself, he followed us to this place.

I felt angry. It was hard to believe Fumikazu once respected him.

Kite glared at Balmung. "You mean . . . you used us?"

"It was necessary to restore order!"

"Order? There's an order that The World desires, and then there's the order that you desire. Which form should it take, Balmung?"

"The order that *I* desire, of course," came a voice out of thin air. Slowly, a figure took shape. He looked down at us, his arms folded. It was Lios!

"Our featured performer. Now all the actors have assembled." Helba smiled.

Lios ignored her and scowled at us. "You pose a grave threat to this world. I'll delete you all!" Lios held out his arm as he had when he deleted Plaird.

Suddenly, the earth rumbled and the screen warped. Lios looked at Helba, bewildered. "What did you do?!"

"I haven't done anything. This is *her* doing. It would appear that she doesn't care for us very much," replied Helba. She laughed scornfully.

"Her?" Kite murmured.

Does she mean Aura?

Before I could ask, Helba turned to us. "Yes. Her. In other words, The World itself."

Then the screen abruptly inverted and the loud shriek erupted again from the speakers. When the screen reverted back to normal, a powerful gust of wind swept over us.

I could see Balmung and Lios warp out before the wind could overtake them. *Wait, are they running away?!*

Helba floated away into the air.

"Wait!" I called, but my voice was drowned out by the wind.

"What's happening?!" Mistral screamed from behind me and Kite.

Did we get left behind?

Yellow hexes appeared on the ground, and just as suddenly as the wind started, it stopped because we had been warped to a new location.

Purple rock clusters floated in the air, and underneath inky black clouds, we saw another irregular creature.

"A leaf?" I murmured.

"Uh-oh, it's not from the strategy guide! It must be another one of those things. Group up!" Mistral cried.

Kite and I ran to her so she could cast strengthening magic on us.

The earth quaked.

"Here it comes!" Kite readied his blades.

The monster slowly floated down from the sky. On either side of its dark green matchstick-like body were giant leaves resembling the shape of canoe oars. I targeted the monster.

Magus. I knew it. Once we beat this thing, there are only five more!

I charged into the fray.

"BlackRose!" Kite called.

I brought my sword up as a shield. The leafy tendrils I'd been fighting suddenly exploded.

Everyone took heavy damage; it nearly killed us.

Mistral used a recovery spell that affected all allies around her.

"Where did it go?"

"Over there!" Mistral pointed.

Magus had lifted into the air, its leafy segments slowly regenerating. At this rate, there would be no end to it!

"All we can do is aim for the body," I muttered, then gritted my teeth.

Kite said, "I'll go after the body. BlackRose, will you take out the leaves? Destroy them before they have a chance to grow back and explode."

"Roger!" I replied.

"I'll handle recovery from the back!" Mistral shouted.

"Here it comes!"

Magus floated back to the ground. It dispersed its leaves, but I made sure to kill each one before they could detonate.

"I can do it!" Kite held out the arm with the bracelet and lined Magus up in the sight.

But one of Magus' leaves had evaded me and slipped near Kite. It exploded!

Defenseless, Kite's HP nearly dropped to zero.

"Kite!" I screamed.

"I'm all right." Kite smiled at me and then activated the data drain. The bracelet lit up, and an arrow of light shot through Magus. Then Kite quickly drank a recovery potion.

Magus had turned to stone. Actually, it resembled nine stones of various sizes, all fused together. I started hacking at it.

Mistral attacked with spells from the rear. "GiRue Kruz!" she cried.

Icicles formed out of the air and pelted Magus. The creature let out a death cry and crumbled.

"I got the last hit!" Mistral said proudly.

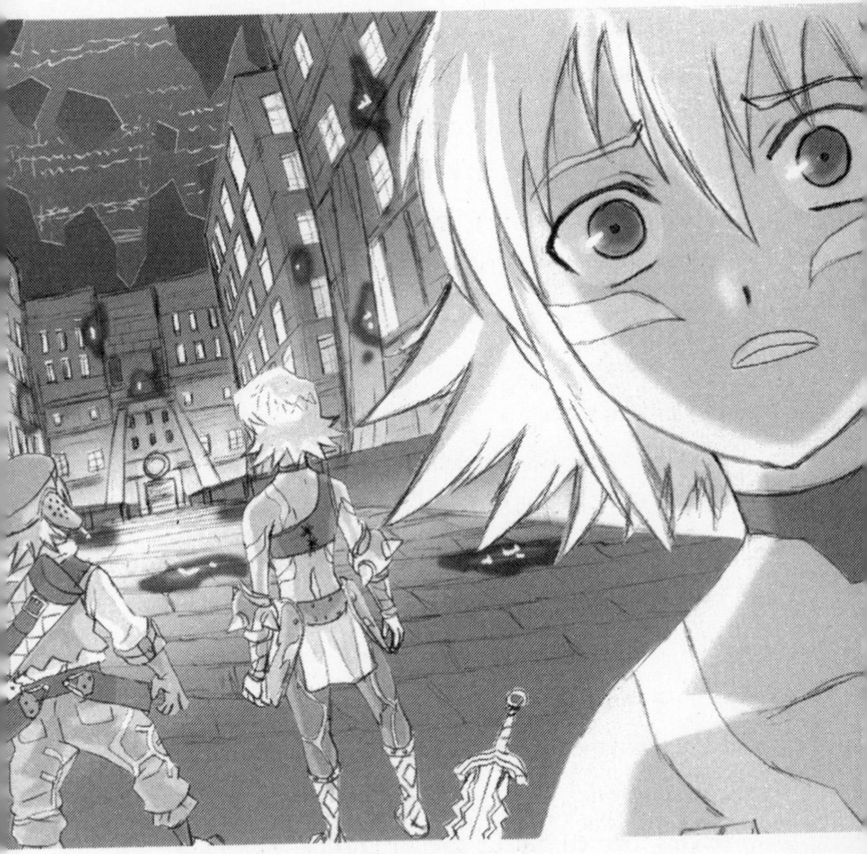

No sooner had she said it than we were warped back to Net Slum. Our feeling of relief was short-lived. The ground rumbled.

Why is there an earthquake, when we defeated it? I thought.

The vibration became even more intense. Suddenly, pieces of debris were sucked into the sky. Gravity itself seemed to be failing. It felt like the end of the world.

"It's falling apart!" I shouted.

"Let's get outta here," said Kite as he warped the party back to town.

Carmina Gadelica wasn't much better. I was speechless as I stared at the once beautiful town. The streets were empty of avatars. The town was covered with scorched stains and crawling yellow character strings. Even the streets of the root town were now contaminated.

"What happened?" Mistral asked, dumbstruck.

"I don't know," I quietly replied.

"I . . . I think we're done for today," Kite said tonelessly, in shock.

Without another word, we disbanded and logged out.

● ⬡ ●

Even after I removed the goggles, I couldn't shake the image of Carmina Gadelica. Then I heard Mom call from downstairs. She sounded insistent. "Akira! Come here!"

I ran down and found her standing in front of the TV.

"It's a news flash from Minato Mirai," she cried. "Your father . . ."

Dad had gone to a conference in Minato Mirai. I stared at the television. Images of rubble and fire covered the screen. I caught the trembling voice of the reporter, "Th-the Minato Mirai district of Yokohama. Few details are known, but right now Yokohama, Sakuragi, Kannai, as well as part of Keihin are under strict traffic regulation, and all commuter rail and subway lines have ceased operating . . ."

I couldn't tell what exactly was happening, but I knew that somewhere, amid all the chaos and confusion, was my father.

To be continued . . .

Postscript

Hello, I'm Waka from CyberConnect2. I oversee the illustrations.

Last time, we printed designs of Akira. So this time, I thought we should introduce some of the people around her.

In *Another Birth*, there are many characters depicted in real life who are not talked about in the game. In volume 2, the confrontation with the three bullying upperclassmen, the exchange with Asaoka, and Hagiya's romantic pursuit make for some interesting developments.

There aren't many illustrations of real life characters, mostly because their roles aren't as significant, but many times throughout the story I found myself wanting to draw them.

I think that individual designs should be done for characters that appear even in the smallest extent, so as to make them memorable. However, if the real-life characters are too unique, they cease to seem realistic. Within the game, characters with hairstyles that could hardly exist in the real world are acceptable, but I think that if it's overdone, then it will lose its impact in the game world.

Miu Kawasaki directed me on character creation. For Risa she described "a girl with very short hair and big eyes." I thought she should be cute and cheerful, something I could easily design. Because her personality had the cutest feel, if I get a chance to illustrate her next time I'd like to draw her expressions.

While Risa and Akira are cheerful, Asaoka and Shouko are quiet. They both have an honor student or liberal arts feel to them. It's difficult finding a way to show individuality in characters like that, so I decided to give Shouko straight hair to show her sense of meekness. Asaoka has wavy hair that's lighter in color. I think she comes across as tender, kind, and frail. At least that's what I tried to express as I designed her.

I think deeply about every character, but when I design I have wild ideas about their everyday lives. It makes the process quite fun.

Art File

.hack // Another Birth

When it comes to characters in the game, there's little to design that hasn't already been done. Chimney is the only original character who doesn't appear in the games. However, both Chimney and Nova appeared so seldom at first that I ended up thinking of them as bit players.

Real World Character Designs

Asaoka is kind, intellectual, and has an "ideal big sister" feel.

●Shouko's design.

This seems an unlikely image for Asaoka.

Art File

I wound up giving Chimney a design that didn't set him apart, since I based him on Albireo from *AI Buster* and simply mixed in some Kite. Now that he's appearing so frequently in the story, I wish I had given him some more individuality.

● Risa's creation.

HI!

I think you'd find Risa and Akira's daily interactions very heart-warming.

I'LL TREAT YOU TODAY.

Risa's overly expressive manner makes her look cute.

● Three upper-classmen bullies.

Nova, on the other hand, actually appears in the games, but he's so dark that I decided to give him a little more color.

Regarding regular game characters, I basically matched up my designs with the original designs, but I think there are also a number of places where my own tastes and subjectivity crept in.

Game World
Character Designs

● Nova's design.

I think Elk's self-doubt is strongly represented.

● Elk's design.

Aromatic Grass. At first I didn't notice.

I wanted to preserve Elk's sense of frailty.

Although there are no illustrations of Chimney fighting, I wanted a cool drawing of him in battle.

● Chimney's design.